Healthyish

Healthyish

A Cookbook with Seriously Satisfying, Truly Simple,
Good-For-You (but Not Too Good-For-You) Recipes for Real Life

Lindsay Maitland Hunt

Photography by Linda Pugliese

Abrams, New York

How to Be Healthyish

The best recipes are like the best people: patient, forgiving, and playful.

Which are the cookbooks you use the most? I'm guessing they're the dirtiest ones on your shelf. Now that this book is in your hands, these recipes can become living, evolving components of your home and kitchen life. Get loose where you feel comfortable, jot your notes in the margins, dog-ear the pages, and mix and match recipes across the book.

I call *Healthyish* cooking "actual cooking." Dreaming of the perfect meal does not get food on the table. We want ingredients we can get at the grocery store, that we can cook in a reasonable amount of time, and that don't leave us with a sink full of dishes. I'm talking recipes for the real world.

Healthyish works if you're just getting started in the kitchen or if you've been at the stove for twenty years because I've developed each recipe with the home cook in mind. My background as a recipe developer for magazines like *Real Simple* and websites like BuzzFeed means that I've spent years creating recipes for busy moms, cash-strapped students, and overworked young professionals. This is a wide group of cooks, but they are all looking for the same thing: doable recipes that taste good, but don't make you feel guilty or weighed down. Not to mention these recipes can't take up too much time or create too many dishes. That's why I asked home cooks (just like you) to test each recipe in this book to make sure that cooks of all skill levels feel welcome here.

HEALTHYISH IS ABOUT

Flexibility

With accessible ingredients,
streamlined recipes, and equipment
you probably already have
in your kitchen, planners and
lovers of the last-minute alike
can cook *Healthyish*.

For me, planning out meals at the beginning of the week liberates me from later stress. But, for others, that could feel like taking away the freedom to choose what you feel like eating for dinner at 5 P.M. *Healthyish* recipes work either way. You can prep them ahead of time, or start right before dinnertime. I created *Healthyish* recipes to fit the lives of many different cooks.

All of this means that, after fifteen minutes of chopping and prep, you can step away from the stove to change into sweats, uncork the wine, and queue up your favorite show on TV while your dinner finishes cooking.

Or, wake up and dig a few things out of your pantry and fridge that will make a casual, filling breakfast in a few minutes, so you can enjoy time with your partner before the day begins. (May I suggest the Cozy Bean and Egg Skillet for Two on page 40?) It's possible to have more luxurious mornings at the breakfast table without panicking about a mound of dishes, or running hungry out the door and straight into an important meeting.

Or, if you have kids, your evening time might be all about feeding your kids and getting them bathed and to bed. You can still squeeze in a quick *Healthyish* dinner with your partner AND get the dishes done before 10 P.M.

Or, if you get home at 8 P.M. after a long day, you can still sit down to a nice meal before 9 P.M.

This way of living is a road map to more time with our people and doing the things we love, all while feeling good about eating tastily. And that is something that anyone could use a little more of.

HEALTHYISH IS ABOUT

Balanced Eating

The thing about balance is that it has become a metric that's another thing we have to live up to. This is personal for me— I've oscillated between extremes my entire life, whether it was eating a greasy grilled cheese or eating a boring bowl of steamed vegetables. But seesawing between the two isn't how you achieve balance.

Healthyish recipes are about having the biggest, most delicious plate of food possible that incorporates vegetables and, yeah, some bacon. It's a big, hearty bowl of food that doesn't leave you feeling weighed down. Food that makes you feel good, and not sad. That's a balanced approach to eating.

Healthyish can mean choosing whole grains instead of refined, packing your plate with vegetables and flavorful ingredients like olives or a few slices of salami for excitement, or simply swapping processed foods like bottled salad dressing for something homemade. It's OK to dollop an extra spoonful of sour cream on a vegetarian chili. Hell, you only live once!

HERE ARE MY FIVE RULES
FOR CREATING A BALANCED MEAL:

ACID, FAT, AND SALT

A good recipe strikes a balance between tart, rich, and salty. Without one, the other two throw the recipe off-kilter.

KEEP IT SIMPLE

Coco Chanel said, "Before you leave the house, look in the mirror and take one thing off." When you buy good ingredients, you don't need to layer on more and more to have a better meal. This is part of my approach to keeping the ingredient list tight; it saves you time and money, and in the end you'll have something more delicious.

COLOR AND BEAUTY

There's a reason we are drawn to bright orange carrots, jewel-toned beets, and neon green lettuce—those colors signify nutrients. So, the more colors of whole foods that you have on your plate, the more nutritious your meal is. Color goes hand in hand with beauty. What looks nice is also appetizing.

FLAVOR BOOSTERS AND FUN

Healthyish recipes incorporate delicious flavor boosters that add pops of excitement to what would be an otherwise bland meal. Crunchy moments in the midst of something soft, and bursts of a contrasting intensity tucked into a simple base like rice are what make *Healthyish* eating satisfying. I'm talking about flaky sea salt, ripe avocados, salty Parmesan, and savory miso paste. Whether it's dotting a shakshuka with crumbles of feta, or folding Marcona almonds and avocado into a roasted vegetable salad, the key is to not be so restrained that your food feels sad.

MAXIMUM VOLUME, MINIMUM CALORIES

When it comes to portion size, I've always felt that more is more. When I see a big plate or bowl filled with food, I anticipate satisfaction. Instead of loading up on calorie-dense foods, *Healthyish* eating relies on vegetables and fruit to increase volume without adding extra calories.

HEALTHYISH IS ABOUT

Recipes That Work

In this age of food blogs and Pinterest, there are millions of recipes available on the Internet. All you need to do is Google "chicken casserole" to find hundreds of options. How do you know which one is the right one to choose? Which one will actually work? And, what does it even mean for a recipe to "work"? There's nothing more disappointing than spending money on hard-to-find ingredients, and investing your precious time, only to end up with an unsatisfying meal.

I've spent eight years testing and creating recipes, surveying everyone I know who eats (so, you know, *literally* everyone I know) and working those observations into my recipes. My goal is to give you good, doable recipes that fit into your real life. To make sure I achieve this, I ask myself these questions:

- Is this something new that doesn't already exist? If this type of recipe does exist, is my recipe a faster, smarter, easier version?

- Are there any extraneous ingredients that I could cut?

- Is there a way to use fewer dishes?

- Is this the most efficient way to do it?

- Can I lighten this up to be healthier?

These are the tenets of *Healthyish* recipes and they are the heart and soul of why I love helping people learn to cook.

CLEAR DESCRIPTIONS

Healthyish recipes are clear about what you're looking for, whether that's "wilted and tender" greens, or a cookie bar whose "edges are starting to pull away from the pan."

ACCURATE VISUAL REFERENCES

Every photo in this book tells the truth about the recipe. I made sure to always include the right serving size and didn't overstyle. Often for the sake of a pretty photo, food stylists will undercook vegetables like a green bean to maintain a fresh green hue, but that's at the expense of the home cook. I want you to look at the picture and know what you are going to get.

STREAMLINED METHOD

All recipes are concise, with a clear order of operations, and don't require using too many pots and pans.

NOTES ABOUT

Equipment, Cook Time, and Ingredients

EQUIPMENT:

The happy truth is that fancy equipment doesn't make you a better cook. With a sharp chef's knife, a cutting board, and a few pans, pots, and bowls, you can make almost anything in this book.

COOK TIME:

I haven't provided overall times for the recipes in the book because everyone's speed and skill level varies. However, within each recipe, I provide ranges of times and indicators for what you should be looking for. In these cases, the indicator should guide you and the time is more of a reference point. For example, if the recipe says "cook, stirring often, until the onions are translucent and soft, 10 to 12 minutes," you're looking for "translucent and soft" and they're likely to be done in 10 to 12 minutes. But! Variables like burner size, pot size, frequency of stirring, or how small or large you've chopped the onion will change the timing.

INGREDIENTS:

I don't want to add stress by including items that aren't easily available at your local grocery store. So, I've created recipes that use ingredients that you're probably familiar with. I'm never going to ask you to get cardoons or an obscure cheese like kashkaval. That being said, there are a few things that may be new to you that are worth it:*

MISO PASTE

Miso is made from fermented soybeans and is high in umami—the so-called fifth taste that translates roughly from Japanese to "savory." I like to think of it as salty, nutty, and adding a "What is that?!" delicious flavor to almost anything it touches. You can find it in the refrigerated section of your grocery store—I like white miso for its balanced flavor and light color, but red or yellow work, too. Many miso pastes contain gluten, so double check the label if you're gluten-free.

TAHINI

Sesame seed paste—you can find it near the nut butters at your grocery store.

FISH SAUCE

An intensely flavorful sauce made from fermented anchovies. My favorite brand is Red Boat.

SMOKED PAPRIKA

Smoked ingredients are a love it or hate it kind of thing. I, personally, love the meaty vibe that smoked paprika lends to anything it touches. Store it in the fridge so it doesn't go rancid.

SARDINES

Look for sustainably caught oil-packed sardines. Split the fillets gently down the middle to pull out the small spine.

DATE MOLASSES

A sweetener made out of dates. Look for it in the baking aisle at your store, or near the maple syrup.

AGAVE NECTAR OR SYRUP

A sweetener made from an agave plant (the same kind used for tequila). I like the clean sweetness it has, perfect for pairing with flavorful ingredients.

BUCKWHEAT FLOUR

A gluten-free flour alternative made from buckwheat, which is actually related to rhubarb! I love it for its nutty, rich flavor.

URFA PEPPER AND ALEPPO PEPPER

These are specialty peppers from Turkey and Syria, respectively. I love their intense savory heat without being too spicy. You can substitute crushed red pepper flakes for a similar, hotter effect.

FLAKY SEA SALT

I keep a small jar of flaky sea salt on my kitchen counter and dining table. I finish every dish with a dusting of flakes for an intense pop of salty flavor and crunchy texture. You can do the same or finish with kosher salt. My favorite brands are Maldon and Jacobsen because they're relatively affordable, but any high-quality salt is worth a try.

*PS I use all these items sparingly, so if you can't find them or don't want to buy them, don't worry about it.

New to the Kitchen?

If you're new to cooking and feeling intimidated, here are my nine key pieces of advice to set yourself up for success.

1 Read the whole recipe before you begin, noting what equipment you'll need. It can be helpful to pull out the pots and pans you'll need to make cooking go smoothly.

2 Be nice to yourself. Maintain a balance of trying new things and giving yourself permission to take it easy.

3 Do any dishes that are in the sink before you start cooking.

4 Prep the ingredients before you start cooking.

5 Cooking gets easier over time. A recipe not coming out as expected is not a reflection of you.

6 If you're making a recipe that calls for the oven to be preheated, do it the second you start prepping. This way, it'll be at the correct temperature and you won't waste time.

7 Put a damp paper towel under your cutting board to secure it to your countertop.

8 Place a mixing bowl on your work area to use as a waste bin for easy cleanup. This way, you won't always have to be reaching for the trash can.

9 Use a bigger cutting board, mixing bowl, or colander than you think you need.

CHAPTER 1

Breakfast

Breakfast tends to be polarizing. No one's ever hating on dinner, but when it comes to breakfast, there are two camps: The "Too Much Work, Can't Be Bothered" camp that waits until lunch, and the "Best Way to Start Your Day" camp. As you may have guessed, I am a love-it-can't-live-without-it breakfast fan.

If you're with me, then you don't need to be convinced of why it's worth it to take some time before work or school starts. (Or even setting aside a weekend afternoon to prep a big batch breakfast.)

For you other guys, if you're even reading this chapter, hear me out. These ideas for breakfast are simply meals. I've eaten muesli and granola for dinner many times—it answers a childlike dessert-for-dinner craving without being too decadent. The morning grain bowls and toasts can be lunch or dinner, and the smoothies and banana bread both easily stand in as an afternoon snack.

←
**Cheddary Corn and
Scallion Muffins**
PAGE 64

Smoothies

There are very few rules to making a great smoothie. In fact, whole books and websites are devoted to them. So, why do you need some new recipes? Well, the truth is, blending a banana with a scoop of fruit and a pour of milk tastes delicious. But, will it keep you full until lunch? Probably not.

THE KEYS TO A GREAT SMOOTHIE ARE:

- Doesn't take a lot of work in the morning
- Has fiber and protein to keep you full
- Has rich flavors—which is why you'll see spices, vanilla, and other potentially "unusual ingredients." These are always optional, but I think make the difference between fine and delicious.
- Sweetness is secondary (not too much fruit, unsweetened nut milks)
- Add the liquid last so that the chunky bits blend first and the smoothie doesn't warm up too much.

The recipes have my suggested liquids and sweetener, but feel free to use whatever you like best or have on hand. Agave, maple syrup, and honey can all be swapped out. Same goes for almond, rice, hemp, and oat milk.

Chocolate and Peanut Butter Smoothie with a Kick

MAKES 1 SMOOTHIE

Who wants to drink a chocolate milkshake for breakfast? [Raises hand.] Unfortunately, that just doesn't fly on a regular basis. Cocoa powder adds a chocolatey flavor with very few calories and no sugar, and peanut butter adds richness and depth. Sometimes, I add ¼ cup quick-cooking oats to this smoothie for extra bulk and fiber. Rolled oats will work, too, if you have a super powerful blender.

INGREDIENTS

- 1 large banana
- ½ cup to 1 cup (120 to 240 ml) ice, depending on how thick you like your smoothie
- 2 tablespoons peanut butter
- 1 tablespoon unsweetened cocoa powder
- 1 teaspoon agave nectar
- ¼ teaspoon ground cinnamon
- ¼ teaspoon pure vanilla extract
- Pinch cayenne pepper
- 1 cup (240 ml) unsweetened almond milk

HOW TO MAKE IT

Combine all the ingredients in your blender, adding the almond milk last. Blend until smooth, and drink right away!

Dairy-Free Tahini, Mango, and Coconut Water "Lassi"

MAKES 1 SMOOTHIE

I love mango lassi, a sweet yogurt drink popular in India. But, since I use dairy as an accent, a yogurt-based smoothie is out of the question. Instead, coconut water acts as a base and plays well with tropical mango.

INGREDIENTS

- 1 cup (165 g) frozen mango
- 1 medium banana
- 1 cup (240 ml) ice
- 2 tablespoons tahini
- ¾ cup (180 ml) coconut water

HOW TO MAKE IT

Combine all the ingredients in your blender, adding the coconut water last. Blend until smooth, and drink right away!

Super-Green Pineapple and Spinach Smoothie

MAKES 1 SMOOTHIE

This smoothie packs a cup of spinach into a well-balanced breakfast. Plus, the pineapple is sweet enough so you don't need any maple syrup.

INGREDIENTS

- 1 small banana
- 1 cup (245 g) frozen pineapple
- 1 cup (155 g) frozen chopped spinach
- 1 tablespoon flaxseeds
- 1½ cups (360 ml) unsweetened almond milk

HOW TO MAKE IT

Combine all the ingredients in your blender, adding the almond milk last. Blend until smooth, and drink right away!

**Banana-Avocado
Chai Shake**
PAGE 26

↑ **Carrot-Pumpkin
Smoothie**
PAGE 27

← **Gingery Peach and
Berry Smoothie**
PAGE 26

**Chocolate and Peanut
Butter Smoothie with a Kick**
PAGE 23 →

Dairy-Free Tahini, Mango,
and Coconut Water "Lassi"
PAGE 23

→

Turmeric-Horchata
Smoothie
PAGE 27

↓

Super-Green
Pineapple and
Spinach Smoothie
PAGE 23

↑

Banana-Avocado Chai Shake

MAKES 1 SMOOTHIE

Given avocado's superstar status in the food world, you'd think that it would be in more smoothies. Not only does it add body and protein, but it also gives smoothies a milkshake–like richness. I first tasted an avocado shake in Morocco, but the multifaceted flavors of Indian chai spice fit even better here. Of course, you can use just cinnamon or a pinch of ground cardamom for a quick fix.

INGREDIENTS

½ cup (120 ml) ice cubes

1 small banana

½ avocado

1 teaspoon agave nectar

1 teaspoon Chai Spice Mix (recipe below)

1 cup (240 ml) unsweetened almond, soy, rice, or hemp milk

HOW TO MAKE IT

Combine all the ingredients in your blender, adding the almond milk last. Blend until smooth, and drink right away!

Chai Spice Mix

MAKES ABOUT ¼ CUP

This is a good time to recycle an old empty spice jar. Rinse and dry it well before using—if it's wet, the spices will clump and mold.

Combine 1 tablespoon each ground cinnamon and ground ginger, 2 teaspoons ground cardamom, and 1 teaspoon each ground cloves and freshly ground black pepper in a small jar. Cover and shake to combine.

The chai spice mix will keep in a jar at room temperature for up to 3 months.

Gingery Peach and Berry Smoothie

MAKES 1 SMOOTHIE

The combination of oats, vanilla, ginger, and berries makes this taste like a summer crisp. I like 100-percent fruit preserves for sweetness without adding straight-up sugar.

INGREDIENTS

1 cup (250 g) frozen peaches

½ cup (75 g) frozen mixed berries

¼ cup (20 g) quick-cooking oats

1 tablespoon berry preserves (no-sugar-added, if possible)

2 teaspoons peeled and grated fresh ginger, or 2 teaspoons fresh ginger juice, or 1 teaspoon ground ginger

¼ teaspoon pure vanilla extract

1½ cups (360 ml) unsweetened almond milk

HOW TO MAKE IT

Combine all the ingredients in your blender, adding the almond milk last. Blend until smooth, and drink right away!

Turmeric-Horchata Smoothie

MAKES 1 SMOOTHIE

Growing up in Los Angeles, I lived on a steady diet of incredible Mexican food. On the side of every meal I drank a frosty glass of horchata—a traditional Mexican cinnamon rice drink. Horchata is made by processing raw white rice with water and steeping until you get a milky liquid. Then it's souped up with massive amounts of sugar and a hefty dose of cinnamon. Naturally, I still love those flavors, but something lighter is more my speed for daily drinking. Turmeric adds color and has anti-inflammatory properties.

INGREDIENTS

- 1 cup (240 ml) ice cubes
- 1 medium banana
- 2 tablespoons almond butter
- 1 teaspoon light agave nectar
- ½ teaspoon ground turmeric
- ¼ teaspoon ground cinnamon
- ¼ teaspoon vanilla extract
- 1 cup (240 ml) unsweetened rice milk

HOW TO MAKE IT

Combine all the ingredients in your blender, adding the rice milk last. Blend until smooth, and drink right away!

Carrot-Pumpkin Smoothie

MAKES 1 SMOOTHIE

This smoothie packs a whopping serving of beta-carotene—which gives both carrots and pumpkins their beautiful orange hues. Beta-carotene converts to vitamin A in our bodies, helping vision and our immune systems, among other benefits. If you don't want to use carrot juice, try swapping in orange or apple juice. But, skip the maple syrup until you taste the smoothie since those juices tend to be on the sweeter side.

INGREDIENTS

- ½ cup (125 g) pumpkin purée
- 1 small banana
- ½ cup (120 ml) ice cubes
- 1 tablespoon flaxseeds
- ¼ teaspoon ground cinnamon
  Pinch nutmeg
- 1 cup (240 ml) fresh carrot juice
- 1 teaspoon maple syrup

HOW TO MAKE IT

Combine all the ingredients in your blender, adding the carrot juice last. Blend until smooth, and drink right away!

Eggs

Not only are eggs an amazing source of protein, they're a versatile ingredient for breakfast. I can eat eggs every day of the week and never get sick of them.

These recipes showcase my favorite ways of making eggs: a soft, custardy scramble, crispy fried eggs, runny yolk 6-minute boiled eggs, not-quite hard-boiled 9-minute eggs, and poaching the eggs directly into a sauce—in this case, saucy, herbed white beans.

A NOTE ABOUT THE WELFARE OF EGG-LAYING CHICKENS IN THE UNITED STATES

The best place to buy eggs is your local farmers' market. Usually this means that the chickens roam free and graze on a mixed diet. In the market, comparable terms are "free range," "certified humane," and "organic." It's easy to get sticker shock in the market when you see the conventional eggs at two or three dollars cheaper per carton; however, those eggs come with a price of their own. A five-dollar carton of organic eggs comes out to fewer than fifty cents per egg, or less than a dollar for a two-egg breakfast.

Pesto-Swirled Scrambled Eggs

MAKES BREAKFAST FOR 1

Restaurant-quality eggs, in your pajamas. Victory! This would work well with any sauce. Try it with olive tapenade or chopped sun-dried tomatoes.

INGREDIENTS

- 2 large eggs
- Kosher salt and freshly ground black pepper
- 1 tablespoon olive oil
- 1 tablespoon pesto (basil is nice, but any other kind will work well)
- 1 large slice whole-wheat bread, toasted
- 1 ounce (about 2 tablespoons/28 g) fresh goat cheese

HOW TO MAKE IT

Get a medium nonstick skillet good and hot over medium-high heat—for at least a minute but not too much longer.

While the skillet heats, use a fork to beat the eggs in a small bowl with ¼ teaspoon salt and a few generous grinds of black pepper.

Pour the oil into the skillet and swirl it to coat the pan. Have a silicone spatula ready, and pour the eggs into the pan. Start stirring immediately in wide swoops, pulling the edges in to the center (they'll start to cook faster). It will take only 1 to 2 minutes to get the eggs to a soft scramble, so don't walk away.

Pull the pan off the heat and swirl in the pesto. Spoon the eggs over the toast and sprinkle with the cheese.

Plain Jane Soft-Scrambled Eggs

MAKES BREAKFAST FOR 1

Making perfect scrambled eggs isn't hard, but a little planning ensures silky, custardy eggs instead of rubbery, overcooked ones. Since the eggs cook in a minute or two, don't start anything until all your ingredients are prepped and measured out. Finish the eggs with Lemony Parsley Butter (page 227) for a fancier take.

INGREDIENTS

- 2 or 3 large eggs
- 2 tablespoons whole milk or heavy cream (optional)
- Kosher salt and freshly ground black pepper
- 1 tablespoon unsalted butter
- Buttered toast and flaky sea salt, for serving

HOW TO MAKE IT

Get a medium nonstick skillet good and hot over medium-high heat—for at least a minute but not too much longer.

While the skillet heats, use a fork to beat the eggs in a small bowl with the milk or cream (if you're using it), ¼ teaspoon salt, and a few generous grinds of pepper.

Add half of the butter to the skillet and swirl it to coat the pan. Have a silicone spatula ready and pour the eggs into the pan. Immediately start stirring in wide swoops, pulling the edges in to the center (they'll start to cook faster). It will take only 1 to 2 minutes to get the eggs to a soft scramble, so don't walk away.

Pull the pan off the heat and stir in the rest of the butter. Serve immediately with toast, topped with flaky sea salt.

Chorizo Breakfast Tacos

MAKES BREAKFAST FOR 1

Just one small piece of dried chorizo sausage adds smoky, meaty flavor to these tacos. You cook the chorizo in a little bit of oil first so each piece gets nice and crispy (plus it seasons the oil, too!). To remove the casing on the chorizo, use your knife to make a thin cut from tip to tip. Grab an edge of the papery skin and pull it off in a firm but steady motion, then slice.

INGREDIENTS

- 2 corn tortillas
- 2 large eggs
  Kosher salt and freshly ground black pepper
- 2 teaspoons olive oil
- 1 (2-in/5-cm) piece dried chorizo, cut into half-moons
- 1 tablespoon chopped fresh flat-leaf parsley, plus more for serving
- 2 tablespoons crumbled Cotija or feta cheese

HOW TO MAKE IT

Using tongs, put a tortilla directly on the grate of a gas burner turned to medium-high. Cook, flipping once, until the edges are charred and the tortilla is hot. Repeat to toast the second tortilla. Keep warm.

Use a fork to beat the eggs in a small bowl with $\frac{1}{8}$ teaspoon salt and a few generous grinds of black pepper. You're looking for them to be uniformly yellow and slightly frothy.

Heat the oil in a medium nonstick skillet over medium heat. Add the chorizo and cook, stirring often, until the pieces are golden brown and crispy, 2 to 3 minutes.

Take the pan off the heat and add the eggs. Have a spatula ready and stir constantly, pulling the edges into the center, until the curds are just set, 15 to 30 seconds (this will happen quicker than normal scrambled eggs because the pan is hot).

Fold in the parsley and cheese. Divide the eggs between the toasted tortillas. Sprinkle with a little extra parsley and eat right away.

Hummus and Avocado Flatbread with a Crispy Fried Egg

MAKES BREAKFAST FOR 1

In my opinion, any fried egg that isn't crispy just isn't doing its job. If you're frying it, fry it. This means cranking up the heat, sliding the egg in when the oil is good and hot, and not being afraid to let the edges get lacy and brown. Follow my method and you'll get it right every time.

INGREDIENTS

- 2 teaspoons olive oil
- 1 large egg
- 3 tablespoons plain hummus
- 1 whole-wheat flatbread, toasted
- ¼ avocado, sliced

  Kosher salt and freshly ground black pepper

  Crushed red pepper flakes and fresh cilantro leaves, for serving

HOW TO MAKE IT

Heat the oil in a small nonstick skillet over medium heat. Add the egg to the skillet, cover, and cook the egg until the edges are crispy and the yolk and whites are set, 2 to 3 minutes.

While the egg cooks, smear the hummus on the toasted flatbread and top with the avocado. Slide the cooked egg on top, then sprinkle with ¼ teaspoon each salt and pepper. Top with some red pepper flakes and cilantro leaves. I also like to drizzle any leftover hot oil from the pan on the flatbread.

Miso-Butter Toast with a Nine-Minute Egg

MAKES BREAKFAST FOR 1

The first time I made this toast, I had no way of knowing I'd become completely obsessed, eating it every morning for two weeks straight. The salty-rich miso butter adds a ton of flavor and pairs perfectly with the creamy egg yolks. I usually top the egg with a sprinkle of salt and pepper, but sometimes I go nuts and drizzle with soy sauce, which is equally delicious. If you don't have miso, mix 1 tablespoon of butter with 1 teaspoon soy sauce. It doesn't have the same richness, but you'll get a similar umami taste.

INGREDIENTS

1 large egg

1 slice of your favorite bread, toasted

1 tablespoon Miso Butter (page 227)

Flaky sea salt and freshly ground black pepper, for serving

HOW TO MAKE IT

Bring a small pot of water to a boil. Using a long-handled spoon, gently lower the egg into the water. Roughly dropping it in can cause the shell to crack on the bottom of the pot.

Turn the heat down to a gentle simmer and set a timer for 9 minutes. Carefully remove the cooked egg and submerge in an ice bath or run under cold water until cool enough to handle. Tap the egg gently on the counter and roll to crack the shell all over. Peel the shell off and then slice the egg crosswise into 5 or 6 slices.

Spread the toast with the miso butter and top with the egg. Season with salt and pepper, eat, and enjoy!

Breakfast Caprese with Soft-Boiled Eggs

MAKES BREAKFAST FOR 1

Soft-boiled eggs perfectly enhance the classic flavors of caprese salad. Make sure to place the eggs on top of the tomato and mozzarella so that when you cut into them the yolk runs all over and makes a sauce. I like the baby basil leaves that come from the inside of a bunch. They taste less earthy and look pretty on your plate.

INGREDIENTS

2 large eggs

3 thin slices (about 2 oz/ 55 g) fresh mozzarella

1 small or medium tomato, thinly sliced

1 teaspoon olive oil

A handful of fresh basil leaves

Kosher salt and freshly ground black pepper

HOW TO MAKE IT

Bring a small pot of water to a boil. Using a long-handled spoon, gently lower the eggs into the water. Roughly dropping them in can cause the shells to crack on the bottom of the pot.

Turn the heat down to a gentle simmer and set a timer for 6 minutes. Carefully remove the cooked egg and submerge in an ice bath or run under cold water until cool enough to handle. Tap the egg gently on the counter and roll to crack the shell all over. Peel the shell off.

Arrange the mozzarella and tomato slices on a plate and nestle the eggs into the center so they're secure. Drizzle with the olive oil, sprinkle with basil, season with salt and pepper, and slice open the eggs so that the yolk runs all over.

Cozy Bean and Egg Skillet for Two

MAKES BREAKFAST FOR 2

This is my favorite way to cook eggs for two—perfect for lazier-than-usual mornings with your special person. Toasted and oiled crusty bread is a luxurious addition for dipping in the yolks and sauce, but this is plenty filling without it. If you're opening a new 15-ounce can of beans to make this, save the extras for a grain bowl or hearty salad.

INGREDIENTS

- 1 tablespoon olive oil
- 1 garlic clove, smashed
- 1 teaspoon fresh thyme leaves, plus more to top the eggs
- 1 cup (260 g) canned cannellini beans, rinsed
- ½ cup (120 ml) water
- Kosher salt and freshly ground black pepper
- 2 to 4 eggs, depending on how hungry you are
- Crusty bread, toasted and oiled, for serving (optional)

HOW TO MAKE IT

Heat the oil in a small skillet over medium-high heat. Add the garlic and thyme and cook until the garlic is fragrant, about 45 seconds. Stir in the beans, water, and ¼ teaspoon each salt and pepper. Turn the heat up to high and cook, stirring here and there and smashing the beans with your spatula, until the beans are saucy and the liquid is creamy, 2 to 4 minutes.

Using your spatula, make wells in the beans—one for each egg. Crack the eggs into the wells one at a time, then cover and cook until the whites are set but the yolks still jiggle when you shake the pan a bit, 1 to 2 minutes.

Taste, garnish with thyme leaves, and season with a little more salt and pepper. Eat right away, with toasted and oiled bread, if you want.

Toasts

In the age of Instagram and Pinterest, it seems that almost anything looks good on a piece of toast. It's important to me that my breakfast—and all meals, really—look pretty. Color signifies nutrients, and if it is beautiful, you'll probably want to eat it. While this is important, function is the first rule of making delicious food, especially when it comes to toast.

START WITH AN ANCHOR

An anchor ensures that whatever you put on top of the toast won't just slide off. This could be jam, ricotta, or a nut butter. I hate lifting something up to take a bite only to have everything fall apart.

MAKE IT EASY TO EAT

Your main ingredient should be sliced or placed in a way that is easy to eat. Last I checked, trying to fit your mouth around a two-inch-high breakfast toast was just not doable or fun.

ADD A LITTLE POP OF FLAVOR AND SWEETNESS

I'll add a drizzle of maple syrup for sweetness or a dusting of chili flakes for heat. The key is an enjoyable breakfast, not a daily pre-work obligation. For that you could just drink protein powder mixed with water.

PB-Deluxe Toast with Coconut and Cinnamon

MAKES 1 TOAST

This is my take on the classic peanut butter and banana combo. Look for a whole-grain fruit-and-nut bread like cranberry-walnut from your local bakery. Or, go for a more decadent version with sliced cinnamon-raisin swirl.

INGREDIENTS

- 1 large slice fruit-and-nut bread, toasted
- 1 tablespoon peanut butter
- ½ small banana, sliced in half lengthwise
- 2 teaspoons sweetened shredded coconut
- Pinch ground cinnamon

HOW TO MAKE IT

Spread the toast with the peanut butter. Nestle the banana into the peanut butter and sprinkle with the coconut and a dusting of cinnamon.

PB-Deluxe Toast with Coconut and Cinnamon
PAGE 43

Double Apple, Mint, and Ricotta Toast
PAGE 47

Avocado, Olive Tapenade, and Cheddar Toast
PAGE 46

← Sesame-Marmalade Toast with Fresh Berries
PAGE 47

↖ Almond Butter Toast with Maple-Drizzled Pear
PAGE 46

Avocado, Olive Tapenade, and Cheddar Toast

MAKES 1 TOAST

I love the triple-threat combination of creamy avocado, salty olive tapenade, and sharp Cheddar. Make this even more filling by topping with a fried egg.

INGREDIENTS

1 large slice whole-grain bread, toasted

1 tablespoon olive tapenade

1 thin slice sharp Cheddar cheese

½ avocado, sliced

1 teaspoon olive oil

Flaky sea salt and crushed red pepper flakes, for serving

HOW TO MAKE IT

Spread the toast with the tapenade. Top with the Cheddar and avocado, pressing down to secure the avocado slices. Drizzle with the oil and sprinkle with flaky sea salt and red pepper flakes.

Almond Butter Toast with Maple-Drizzled Pear

MAKES 1 TOAST

Chia seeds are great for adding extra protein to your breakfast, not to mention they add a nice crunch to this toast.

INGREDIENTS

1 large slice rustic sourdough bread, toasted

2 tablespoons almond butter

1 tablespoon chia seeds, plus more for sprinkling

½ ripe pear, thinly sliced

1 teaspoon pure maple syrup

HOW TO MAKE IT

Spread the toast with the almond butter and sprinkle with 1 tablespoon of the chia seeds. Nestle the pear in the almond butter. Drizzle with the maple syrup and sprinkle with more chia seeds.

Sesame-Marmalade Toast with Fresh Berries

MAKES 1 TOAST

Tahini has an earthy flavor that some people find too strong. If that's you, try cashew butter instead.

INGREDIENTS

1 large slice whole-wheat bread, toasted

2 tablespoons orange marmalade, preferably 100-percent fruit

2 tablespoons tahini

½ cup raspberries and blueberries

1 teaspoon sesame seeds

HOW TO MAKE IT

Spread the toast with the marmalade and drizzle with 1 tablespoon of the tahini. Top with the berries, pressing down to secure them. Drizzle with the remaining 1 tablespoon tahini and sprinkle with the sesame seeds.

Double Apple, Mint, and Ricotta Toast

MAKES 1 TOAST

Most commercially made ricotta has stabilizers and is spongy, not creamy. So, if you can find ricotta at your farmers' market or specialty food shop, it's worth the splurge. Since you'll only use a little for the toast, a small container will go a long way.

INGREDIENTS

1 large slice multigrain bread, toasted

3 tablespoons ricotta cheese

1 tablespoon apple butter

½ sweet apple, such as Fuji or Pink Lady, thinly sliced

1 teaspoon agave nectar or pure maple syrup

1 tablespoon small fresh mint leaves

HOW TO MAKE IT

Spread the toast with the ricotta and then gently smear the apple butter on top. Nestle the apple in the apple butter. Drizzle with the agave and top with the mint leaves.

Eight Morning Grain Bowls

OK, step one is picking your favorite grain from page 236. I like to make one big batch for the week, and then mix up the toppings.

I'll leave it to you to choose what to go with what. I'm not a big fan of quinoa with sweet things, but if that's your jam, go wild.

Step two is picking which bowl you're going to make. I tend to get in a groove with one combo and will eat it until I hate it, but you could mix it up—pairing one with each day of the week.

I'll be real with you—these aren't quick breakfasts unless you've made the grains in advance. But if you've done that, one batch will last you a couple days.

My go-to liquid for saucy breakfast bowls is unsweetened almond milk, but you can use any milk you like.

The Why-Didn't-I-Think-of-That Bowl

MAKES BREAKFAST FOR 1

This combination is both obvious and totally new. You're welcome.

INGREDIENTS

- ¾ cup cooked whole grains (I like brown rice best here)
- ½ cup (120 ml) unsweetened almond milk
- 2 tablespoons smooth peanut butter, or any nut butter
- ½ small sweet apple, such as Fuji or Pink Lady, chopped
- 2 teaspoons raw honey
- 1 tablespoon sesame seeds
- 1 tablespoon poppy seeds

HOW TO MAKE IT

Stir the whole grains and almond milk together in a small serving bowl and microwave them until hot. Top with the peanut butter and apple. Drizzle with the honey and sprinkle with the sesame and poppy seeds.

Summer in a Bowl

MAKES BREAKFAST FOR 1

Peaches are one of the few remaining truly seasonal ingredients. It's a ripe, summer peach or no peach. And that is truly wonderful.

INGREDIENTS

- ¾ cup cooked whole grains (I like brown rice best here)
- ½ cup (120 ml) almond milk
- 1 small peach, chopped
- ½ cup (75 g) blueberries
- 1 tablespoon pure maple syrup
- ¼ cup (30 g) slivered almonds, toasted

HOW TO MAKE IT

Stir the whole grains and almond milk together in a small serving bowl and microwave them until hot. Top with the peach and blueberries. Drizzle with the maple syrup and sprinkle with the almonds.

My California BB
Bowl
PAGE 55
↓

←
The Grown-Up
Kid Bowl
PAGE 54

I Dream of Hawaii Bowl

MAKES BREAKFAST FOR 1

When I eat this on cold winter mornings, I close my eyes and imagine myself sitting beachside in Hawaii. It doesn't actually work, but at least I'm enjoying a delicious breakfast.

INGREDIENTS

- ¾ cup cooked whole grains (I like oats best here)
- ½ cup (120 ml) almond milk
- 1 cup (165 g) chopped mango, from 1 ripe mango
- 2 tablespoons pure maple syrup
- ¼ cup (30 g) roasted, unsalted cashews
- 3 tablespoons unsweetened shredded coconut

HOW TO MAKE IT

Stir the whole grains and almond milk together in a small serving bowl and microwave them until hot. Top with the mango. Drizzle with the maple syrup and sprinkle with the cashews and coconut.

The FACT Bowl

MAKES BREAKFAST FOR 1

We're starting a new thing. It's called FACT and it stands for Fried Egg, Avocado, Corn, and Tomatoes. Get on it.

INGREDIENTS

- 1 tablespoon olive oil
- 1 large egg
- ¾ cup cooked whole grains (I like farro best here)
- ½ cup (75 g) fresh corn kernels
- ½ avocado, diced
  A handful of cherry tomatoes, halved or quartered if large
  Flaky sea salt and freshly ground black pepper

HOW TO MAKE IT

Heat the oil in a small nonstick skillet over medium heat. Add the egg, cover, and cook, sunny-side up, until slightly runny, 2 to 3 minutes.

Microwave the grains in a small serving bowl until just barely warm. Stir in the corn, avocado, and tomatoes. Top with the egg and any oil left in the pan. Season with flaky sea salt and a few grinds fresh pepper.

More is more: Pack your plate or bowl with vegetables for extra volume.

An Unapologetically Mushy Breakfast Bowl

MAKES BREAKFAST FOR 1

If you get grossed out by mushy food, then this isn't for you. But, if mushy food makes you feel like you're crawling into a warm blanket fireside (ahem, me!), then get right to it.

INGREDIENTS

- 1 cup cooked whole grains (I like oats best here)
- ½ cup (120 ml) unsweetened almond milk
- 1 cup Roasted Apples (page 67)
- 2 tablespoons peanut butter
- 1 tablespoon pure maple syrup

HOW TO MAKE IT

Stir the whole grains and almond milk together in a small serving bowl and microwave them until hot. Pile the roasted apples on top, then dot with the peanut butter and drizzle with the maple syrup.

The Grown-Up Kid Bowl

MAKES BREAKFAST FOR 1

Bananas on oatmeal were a staple in my house growing up. I still love them together, but adding tart raspberries, crunchy chia seeds, and mint leaves makes this feel refreshingly adult.

INGREDIENTS

- ¾ cup cooked whole grains (I like barley best here)
- ½ cup (120 ml) unsweetened almond milk
- 1 small banana, sliced
- ½ cup (60 g) raspberries
- 1 tablespoon agave nectar or maple syrup
- 1 tablespoon chia seeds
- 1 tablespoon small, fresh mint leaves (tear the leaves if yours are large)

HOW TO MAKE IT

Stir the whole grains and almond milk together in a small serving bowl and microwave them until hot. Top with the banana and raspberries. Drizzle with the agave and sprinkle with the chia seeds and mint leaves.

My California BB Bowl

MAKES BREAKFAST FOR 1

There's a food revolution going on in my hometown, Los Angeles, and sometimes I wish I could live in California to be a part of it. This is inspired by food I've eaten at both Sqirl and Gjusta, two of the most popular restaurants in 2017.

INGREDIENTS

- ¾ cup cooked whole grains, (I like brown rice best here)
- 1 large egg
- 1 cup baby arugula leaves
- ⅓ cup Cucumber-Dill Tzatziki (page 234)

  Olive oil, fresh dill leaves, flaky sea salt, and Aleppo pepper, for serving

HOW TO MAKE IT

Bring a small pot of water to a boil. Using a long-handled spoon, gently lower the egg into the water. Roughly dropping it in can cause the shell to crack on the bottom of the pot.

Turn the heat down to a gentle simmer and set a timer for 9 minutes. Carefully remove the cooked egg and submerge in an ice bath or run under cold water until cool enough to handle. Tap the egg gently on the counter and roll to crack the shell all over. Peel the shell off and then slice the egg crosswise into 5 or 6 slices.

Microwave the grains in a small serving bowl until just barely warm. Top with the egg, arugula, and tzatziki. Drizzle with a little olive oil and sprinkle with dill leaves, flaky sea salt, and Aleppo pepper.

Perfect Pear and Pistachio Bowl

MAKES BREAKFAST FOR 1

This bowl feels like my fancier best friend who somehow always looks stylish AND understated at the same time. #bowlgoals

INGREDIENTS

- ¾ cup cooked whole grains (I like barley best here)
- ½ cup (120 ml) Greek yogurt
- ½ ripe pear, thinly sliced
- 1 tablespoon pure maple syrup
- 1 to 2 tablespoons roasted chopped pistachios

HOW TO MAKE IT

Microwave the grains in a small serving bowl until just barely warm. (You can also eat them cold or at room temperature.) Dollop the yogurt over the grains and then nestle the pear on top. Drizzle with the maple syrup and sprinkle with the pistachios.

Big Batch Breakfasts

You can divide most cooks into two categories: those who like to prep ahead, and those who would rather decide what to eat spontaneously.

My theory: spending an hour or two on a Saturday or Sunday can make both camps happy. Get-ahead types will have breakfast set for the week, and lovers of the last-minute get more time for adventures, in the kitchen or otherwise.

Seeded Whole-Wheat Banana Bread

MAKES ONE 8½ × 4½-INCH (22 × 12-CM) LOAF

I absolutely LOVE banana bread, but so often it's as sweet as a cake and too oily. That's good for special occasions, but for weekday mornings, I want a slice that feels mostly wholesome. That's the "ish" in *Healthyish*.

INGREDIENTS

- ½ cup (120 ml) neutral-flavored oil, such as canola, vegetable, or grapeseed, plus more for the pan
- 1½ cups (6.4 oz/190 g) whole-wheat flour, spooned and leveled, plus more for the pan
- ¼ cup (35 g) plus 2 teaspoons poppy seeds
- ¼ cup (46 g) plus 2 teaspoons sesame seeds
- ⅔ cup (135 g) plus 1 tablespoon granulated sugar
- 2 teaspoons baking powder
- ½ teaspoon kosher salt
- 1 cup mashed banana, from about 3 really ripe bananas
- 2 large eggs, at room temperature
- 1 teaspoon pure vanilla extract
- 1 cup (4 oz/120 g) pecans or walnuts, toasted and chopped (see tip on page 242)

HOW TO MAKE IT

Preheat your oven to 350°F (175°C). Oil and flour a 8½ by 4½-inch (22 by 12-cm) baking pan and set aside.

Mix together 2 teaspoons each of the poppy and sesame seeds and 1 tablespoon of the sugar. Set aside.

In a medium bowl, whisk together the flour, the remaining ¼ cup each of the poppy and sesame seeds, the baking powder, and salt.

In a large bowl, whisk together the banana, eggs, oil, the remaining ⅔ cup (135 g) sugar, and the vanilla. Fold in the dry ingredients until just combined. Stir in the pecans or walnuts. Scrape the batter into the prepared pan and smooth out the top. Sprinkle the reserved poppy-sesame-sugar mixture evenly over the top of the batter.

Bake for 50 to 60 minutes, until a toothpick inserted in the center of the loaf comes out with just a few crumbs attached. Cool for 15 minutes in the pan, then turn onto a rack to cool completely. If you feel comfortable, carefully invert the loaf over the sink to catch any loose seeds and sugar.

The loaf will keep at room temperature, well wrapped, for 3 days. To freeze the loaf, cut it into ¾-inch-thick (2 cm) slices. Put in a zip-top bag with a piece of parchment paper between each slice.

Peanut Butter Granola

MAKES 14 CUPS; SERVES 12 TO 16

Most granolas have the same amount of sugar as a cookie, which means that I leave breakfast feeling guilty that I ate my dessert before even starting the day. So, I developed this recipe with as little sweetener as possible—a serving has only 2 teaspoons of maple syrup—just enough to have an indulgent sweetness, but not so much you're sugar-crashing on your commute.

INGREDIENTS

- 1 cup (260 g) smooth, unsweetened peanut butter (preferably natural)
- ⅔ cup (155 ml) pure maple syrup
- ½ cup (120 ml) canola oil
- 2 teaspoons pure vanilla extract
- 1 teaspoon ground cinnamon
- 1 teaspoon kosher salt
- 3 packed cups (12 oz/340 g) old-fashioned rolled oats
- 3 packed cups (11 oz/310 g) quick-cooking oats
- 2 cups (10.5 oz/300 g) unsalted peanuts, half roughly chopped

  Almond milk (or another milk you like) and fresh fruit, for serving

HOW TO MAKE IT

Preheat your oven to 300°F (150°C), with racks positioned in the top and bottom thirds of the oven.

Whisk the peanut butter, maple syrup, oil, vanilla, cinnamon, and salt in a large bowl until smooth. Add both oats and the peanuts and stir with a spatula to combine.

Divide the granola evenly between two rimmed baking sheets and spread with the spatula into a flat layer. Bake for 40 to 45 minutes, rotating the baking sheets front to back and top to bottom halfway through, until the granola is dry looking and beginning to turn golden brown. Do not stir! (This ensures you'll have big chunks of granola.)

Cool completely on the baking sheets and then transfer to an airtight container or zip-top bag. The granola will keep at room temperature for up to 2 weeks, or up to 2 months in the freezer. Serve with almond milk and fresh fruit. I like apples or fresh strawberries.

Toasted Coconut Muesli

MAKES 14 CUPS; SERVES 12 TO 16

Traditional muesli is not toasted and you don't add sweetener until serving. So, this recipe is more like a lightly-sugared granola—there's just ½ cup (120 ml) maple syrup spread over 12 to 16 servings. Call it what you will, a serving of this recipe is packed with coconut, pumpkin seeds, and almonds that have a boatload of protein and fiber. The best part about muesli is that you can soak it overnight for a "porridge-y" breakfast. All you have to do in the morning is top it with fruit.

INGREDIENTS

- ½ cup (120 ml) pure maple syrup
- ½ cup (120 ml) neutral-flavored oil, such as canola, vegetable, or grapeseed
- 1 teaspoon kosher salt
- ½ teaspoon ground ginger
- ¼ teaspoon ground nutmeg
- 4 packed cups (14 oz/400 g) quick-cooking oats
- 2 packed cups (8 oz/225 g) old-fashioned rolled oats
- 2 cups (8 oz/225 g) sliced almonds
- 2 cups (4 oz/115 g) unsweetened coconut flakes (the wide, flat kind)
- 1 cup (5 oz/130 g) pumpkin seeds

  Almond milk (or another milk you like) and fresh fruit, for serving

HOW TO MAKE IT

Preheat your oven to 350°F (175°C), with racks positioned in the top and bottom thirds of the oven.

Whisk the maple syrup, oil, salt, ginger, and nutmeg in a small bowl. Using your hands or a spatula, mix both oats, the almonds, coconut, and pumpkin seeds in a large bowl. Pour the liquids onto the oat mixture and mix until the oats and nuts are well coated.

Divide the muesli evenly between two rimmed baking sheets and smooth into a flat layer. Bake for 15 to 20 minutes, rotating the baking sheets front to back and top to bottom halfway through, until the coconut and almonds are golden brown and the edges of the pan are slightly dark. Do not stir! (This ensures that you'll have big chunks of muesli.)

Cool completely on the baking sheets and then transfer to an airtight container or zip-top bag. The muesli will keep at room temperature for up to 2 weeks, or up to 2 months in the freezer.

To soak the muesli overnight: *Mix equal parts muesli and almond milk in a serving bowl. Cover and refrigerate overnight. Serve topped with fruit.*

To eat right away: *Serve the muesli with almond milk and your favorite fruit.*

Cheddary Corn and Scallion Muffins

MAKES 12 MUFFINS

These muffins have everything I love about cornbread, with corn kernels to bulk up the batter, whole-wheat flour for moderation, and Cheddar for sharp, cheesy flavor.

INGREDIENTS

- ½ cup (1 stick) unsalted butter, melted and cooled to room temperature, plus more for the pan
- ¾ cup (180 ml) whole milk
- 2 large eggs
- 1¼ cups (155 g) whole-wheat flour
- 1 cup (180 g) fine-grind cornmeal
- 1 tablespoon baking powder
- 1 teaspoon granulated sugar
- 2 teaspoons kosher salt
- 1½ teaspoons Aleppo pepper, or ½ teaspoon crushed red pepper flakes
- 2 cups (290 g) frozen corn kernels, thawed
- 1 cup (55 g) scallions, sliced, from 1 small bunch
- 1 cup (about 4 oz/115 g) grated extra-sharp Cheddar cheese

HOW TO MAKE IT

Preheat your oven to 425°F (220°C). Butter a nonstick muffin pan, or butter and flour a regular muffin pan.

In a small bowl, whisk together the milk, eggs, and butter. In a large bowl, whisk together the flour, cornmeal, baking powder, sugar, salt, and Aleppo pepper. Whisk in the milk mixture and then fold in the corn, scallions, and ½ cup of the cheese.

Divide the batter evenly among the prepared muffin cups, then sprinkle with the remaining cheese. Bake until golden brown and a toothpick inserted in the center of a muffin comes out clean, 20 to 25 minutes. Cool in the pan for 5 minutes, then transfer to a rack to cool completely.

Store the muffins at room temperature in an airtight container for up to 3 days. You can also freeze the muffins in a zip-top bag for up to 1 month.

Goldilocks Big-Batch Rolled Oats

MAKES 4 CUPS

Rolled oats are a classic breakfast staple, but often they're too dry and clumpy or overcooked and soupy. This method is somewhat slower than you might be used to, but the consistency is just right every time.

INGREDIENTS

4 cups (960 ml) water

2 cups (180 g) rolled oats

HOW TO MAKE IT

Bring the water to a boil in a large saucepan. Add the oats and return the water to a boil. Reduce to a strong simmer and cook, stirring constantly, until the oats are tender with distinct grains in a creamy liquid, 6 to 8 minutes. If the water starts to foam aggressively, turn down the heat and stir quickly. Once it calms down, turn the heat back up.

Serve right away, or cool and transfer to an airtight container. The oats will keep, refrigerated, for up to 5 days.

Roasted Apples

MAKES 4 CUPS

I started making these roasted apples when I realized that raw apple can be tough on digestion for not just me, but many other people! Not only does this recipe give you the flavors of apple pie, but you also get to eat juicy, delicious apples throughout the week, pre-prepped and ready to go. These are perfect on any sort of sweet breakfast grain bowl (page 48). I also love them paired with a scoop of frozen yogurt or assembled into a parfait with Peanut Butter Granola (page 60) and Greek yogurt.

INGREDIENTS

- 5 apples (about 2½ lbs/1.13 kg total), a mix of any varieties, sliced ¼ inch (6 mm) thick
- ¼ cup (60 ml) water
- 2 tablespoons unsalted butter, cut into small pieces
- 2 tablespoons light or dark brown sugar
- 1 cinnamon stick or 1 teaspoon ground cinnamon
- 1 tablespoon apple cider vinegar
- 2 teaspoons pure vanilla extract

HOW TO MAKE IT

Preheat your oven to 425°F (220°C).

Combine all the ingredients in a 9 by 13-inch (20 by 30-cm) baking dish and toss well so that the apples are coated evenly with the sugar and spices.

Cover with aluminum foil and bake for 25 to 30 minutes, until the apples are tender and saucy. Remove the foil and bake for 10 minutes more, or until the apples are golden brown at the edges and you can pierce a slice easily with a fork. Eat hot or cool completely. Refrigerate in an airtight container for up to 1 week.

CHAPTER 2

Snacks

What I love about a good snack is that it operates outside the boundaries of a normal meal. We're not looking for a "well-rounded" combination of protein, starch, and vegetables; we're looking for delicious.

A snack could be a protein-packed energy bite made special with chocolate and coconut (page 70), or a pile of salty-sour chips dipped in tzatziki (page 234), but either way, a snack is an opportunity for a tasty pause mid-morning or in the late afternoon.

The snack category is one of the fastest growing sectors of prepared and packaged foods, but it's well worth making the time to make your own snack. You can control the amount of salt and sugar (two ingredients that are scarily high in many store-bought snacks) and in the long run, making your own snacks will save you money.

←
Not-Your-Average
Trail Mix
PAGE 73

Truly Delicious Energy Bites

MAKES 12 BITES

These are a mish-mash of all the traditional foods in energy bars—nut butter, coconut, chia seeds, raisins, and oats. The secret to making these satisfying, not sad, is a generous dose of dark chocolate and a roll in pretty, white coconut.

INGREDIENTS

- ½ cup (3 oz/85 g) bittersweet chocolate chips
- ½ cup (120 ml) smooth, unsweetened peanut butter (preferably natural)
- 1¼ packed cups (140 g) unsweetened finely shredded coconut
- ¾ packed cup (75 g) quick-cooking oats
- ½ cup (75 g) golden raisins, separated if they're clumped up
- ¼ cup (25 g) unsweetened cocoa powder
- 3 tablespoons chia seeds
- Kosher salt

HOW TO MAKE IT

Put the chocolate chips and peanut butter in a large, microwave-safe bowl. Microwave in 15-second bursts, stirring, until melted and smooth. Add ¾ cup (85 g) of the coconut, the oats, raisins, cocoa powder, chia seeds, and ¼ teaspoon salt. Using a spatula or your hands, work the mixture together until just barely sticky and everything is incorporated.

Line a baking sheet with parchment paper and set aside. Spread the remaining ½ cup (55 g) coconut on a plate. Scoop twelve 2-tablespoon mounds of the dough and roll each into a ball. Roll the balls one at a time in the coconut. Place on the prepared baking sheet, and use your fingers to flatten each ball into a puck about ¾ inch (2 cm) thick. (If you have a 1-ounce/28-g cookie scoop, this is a faster, easier way to make the balls.)

Refrigerate for at least 30 minutes and then transfer to an airtight container. The bites will keep for up to 5 days in your refrigerator.

Not-Your-Average Trail Mix

MAKES ABOUT 6 CUPS

My goal when creating this trail mix was to land on a combination that I'd never eaten before. Not only is this unique, but it is also truly delicious. Pre-chopped apricots and ginger are key here—if you slice whole, dried ones, they tend to sweat in the jar and make the nuts and seeds soft. However, if that's all you can find, make sure to store the trail mix in the freezer to keep it snappy.

INGREDIENTS

- 2 cups (9 oz/225 g) roasted, unsalted cashews
- 2 packed cups (about 1 lb/445 g) chopped dried apricots
- 1 cup (6 oz/165 g) white chocolate chips
- 1 cup (5 oz/130 g) raw pumpkin seeds
- ½ cup (102 g) chopped crystallized ginger

HOW TO MAKE IT

If you buy raw cashews, toast at 350°F (175°C) for 8 to 10 minutes. Cool completely before proceeding with the recipe. If they're warm at all, they'll melt the chocolate and cause the apricots to sweat.

Toss all the ingredients together in a large bowl. Transfer to a large airtight container, or individual serving containers. The trail mix will keep for up to 2 weeks. Store in the freezer to keep it crisp.

Cucumbers with Harissa-Yogurt Dip

MAKES 1 SNACK

This dip scales up easily for a party hors d'oeuvre. When I put it out for guests, I finish it off with some Aleppo pepper and sesame seeds.

INGREDIENTS

- ¼ cup (60 ml) Greek yogurt
- 1 teaspoon olive oil, plus more for drizzling
  Flaky sea salt and freshly ground black pepper
- 1 teaspoon harissa paste
- 2 or 3 Persian cucumbers, ends trimmed, cut into quarters lengthwise

HOW TO MAKE IT

Mix the yogurt, oil, ¼ teaspoon salt, and a few grinds of pepper together in a small bowl. Stir in the harissa, leaving some streakiness. Drizzle with a little more oil and sprinkle with salt and pepper.

Dip the cucumbers in and eat right away, or make up to 1 day in advance and keep refrigerated until ready to eat.

Spicy Sardines and Hummus on Rice Crackers

MAKES 1 SNACK

The optional parsley and lemon add freshness and a bright kick, but it's not totally practical for a work snack—so feel free to omit them if you want.

INGREDIENTS

- ¼ cup (60 g) plain hummus
- 2 long, flat rice crackers or rice cakes
- 1 (4.25-oz/124-g) tin oil-packed sardines, preferably marinated with chiles
  Fresh flat-leaf parsley leaves (optional), crushed red pepper flakes, and flaky sea salt
- 1 lemon wedge (optional)

HOW TO MAKE IT

Spread the hummus on the crackers. Using your fingers, gently open the sardines and pull out the spine. Place them skin side up on the hummus. Sprinkle with parsley (if using), red pepper flakes, flaky sea salt, a squeeze of lemon juice (if using), and a drizzle of the oil from the sardine tin.

Chips with Tzatziki and Tomatoes

MAKES 1 SNACK

Just a few ingredients make the perfect marriage of tangy and salty, creamy and crunchy.

INGREDIENTS

- ¼ cup Cucumber-Dill Tzatziki (page 234)
- ½ cup (70 g) grape tomatoes, halved lengthwise or cut into quarters if large
  Flaky sea salt and freshly ground black pepper
- 1 ounce (28 g) kettle-cooked potato chips, plain or salt and vinegar

HOW TO MAKE IT

Put the tzatziki in a small bowl and top with the tomatoes. Sprinkle with salt and pepper and serve with the potato chips.

**Chips with Tzatziki
and Tomatoes**

**Cucumbers with
Harissa-Yogurt Dip**

**Spicy Sardines
and Hummus on
Rice Crackers**

Salty Watermelon, Feta, Mint, and Avocado Salad

MAKES 1 GENEROUS SNACK

This snack is the epitome of maximum volume, minimum calories—one of the guidelines for *Healthyish* eating. And, while it's cheaper to buy a watermelon and chop it up yourself, sometimes I treat myself to precut watermelon to speed up prep time. If you want to transport this to work or school, make it entirely but keep the avocado off to the side until you're ready to eat. Drizzle the avocado with a bit of lime juice and press plastic wrap directly on the surface.

INGREDIENTS

- 2 cups (12 oz/340 g) peeled watermelon, cut into ½-inch (12-mm) cubes
- 1 tablespoon fresh lime juice, plus 1 teaspoon lime zest
- 1 teaspoon olive oil

  Flaky sea salt and freshly ground black pepper
- ½ avocado, cut into large dice
- 1 tablespoon crumbled feta cheese
- 1 tablespoon torn fresh mint leaves

HOW TO MAKE IT

Toss the watermelon, lime juice, oil, ¼ teaspoon salt, and a few grinds of pepper in a small bowl. Top with the avocado, cheese, mint, and zest. Sprinkle with more salt and pepper and eat.

Ants on a Date

MAKES 1 GENEROUS SNACK

Remember ants on a log, those celery sticks spread with peanut butter and topped with raisins? I can get behind the PB and raisins part, but celery!? Come on. Instead, I swap the celery for dates and add a dusting of cinnamon.

INGREDIENTS

- 4 or 5 plump Medjool or Deglet Noor dates
- 2 tablespoons peanut butter or another nut butter
- 1 tablespoon golden raisins
- Pinch ground cinnamon

HOW TO MAKE IT

Split the dates open lengthwise. Remove the pits if they're not already pitted. Spread the peanut butter inside the dates, dividing it equally. Top with the raisins, pressing in to anchor them in the peanut butter, and sprinkle with the cinnamon.

Eat right away, or keep at room temperature for up to 12 hours.

Rye Crackers with Goat Cheese and Sliced Pear

MAKES 1 SNACK

Pepper on pear, so underrated.

INGREDIENTS

- 2 to 3 ounces (55 to 85 g) fresh goat cheese
- 2 long and thin rye crackers, such as Wasa
- ½ ripe pear, sliced ¼ inch thick (6 mm) vertically from stem to stem
- Drizzle of honey
- Flaky sea salt and freshly ground black pepper

HOW TO MAKE IT

Spread the cheese on the crackers, dividing it equally. Top with the pear slices, pushing down so they are anchored in the cheese. Drizzle with honey and sprinkle with salt and pepper.

Stock your fridge with flavor boosters like green olives, salty Parmesan, and dried chorizo.

Apple Slice "Cookies"

I'm not into pretending something is a dessert when really it's a piece of fruit with stuff on it. So, I'm not calling these dessert. I'm calling them a snack, and one of the most delicious ones in this chapter at that.

EACH MAKES 1 SNACK

Yogurt and Peanut Butter Granola

INGREDIENTS

1   small, sweet apple, such as Fuji or Pink Lady

¼   cup (60 ml) Greek yogurt

⅓   cup Peanut Butter Granola (page 60)

HOW TO MAKE IT

Cut the apple horizontally into 4 or 5 slices. Poke the seeds out or cut out the center with a small biscuit cutter. Spread each slice with the yogurt, then top with the granola.

Apricot Jam, Toasted Coconut, and Pistachios

INGREDIENTS

1   small, tart apple, such as Granny Smith

2   tablespoons apricot jam

2   tablespoons sweetened shredded coconut

2   tablespoons chopped pistachios

HOW TO MAKE IT

Cut the apple horizontally into 4 or 5 slices. Poke the seeds out or cut out the center with a small biscuit cutter. Spread each slice with the jam, then top with the coconut and pistachios.

Almonds, Raisins, and Cream Cheese

INGREDIENTS

1   small, sweet apple, such as Fuji or Pink Lady

3   tablespoons cream cheese, softened

1   tablespoon sliced almonds

2   tablespoons raisins

Drizzle of honey

HOW TO MAKE IT

Cut the apple horizontally into 4 or 5 slices. Poke the seeds out or cut out the center with a small biscuit cutter. Spread each slice with the cream cheese, then top with the almonds, raisins, and a drizzle of honey.

CHAPTER 3

Lunch

No matter how you feel about the events that fill your day, lunch is an opportunity for a bright spot between meetings, classes, or errands. Too often that means picking up an expensive salad that leaves you feeling hungry only an hour later; not to mention, it has set you back ten dollars or more. It's true that bringing lunches to work takes a little planning, but the payoff is well worth it. The following fall into two categories, tartines and no-cook lunches.

←
Summer Barley Bowl with Chorizo, Cucumbers, and Corn
PAGE 96

Tartines

What differentiates a tartine from a toast? Well, truthfully, not much. But I like how tartine sounds, and for the purposes of *Healthyish*, it means a lunch toast. Savory, filling, and truly delicious.

When I pack a tartine for lunch, I toast the bread in the morning and store each component in a small container, then assemble at work.

← **Turkey, Apple, and Brie Baguette**
PAGE 86

↑ **Smoked Salmon on Rye with Dill-and-Caper Yogurt Schmear**
PAGE 86

← **Tangy Chicken Salad Tartine**
PAGE 87

Smoked Salmon on Rye with Dill-and-Caper Yogurt Schmear

MAKES LUNCH FOR 1

I love the briny capers in the yogurt schmear, but if you want to make this even quicker, sub in the tzatziki on page 234 for the yogurt schmear.

INGREDIENTS

- ¼ cup (60 ml) Greek yogurt
- 1 tablespoon chopped capers
- 1 tablespoon chopped fresh dill
  Freshly ground black pepper
- 1 slice dark rye bread
- 2 ounces (55 g) smoked salmon
  Lemon wedge and flaky sea salt, for serving

HOW TO MAKE IT

In a small bowl, mix together the yogurt, capers, dill, and ⅛ teaspoon pepper. Spread on the bread and top with the smoked salmon. Squeeze the lemon over the salmon and then sprinkle the flaky sea salt, a few grinds of pepper, and more chopped dill over the top. Eat right away.

Turkey, Apple, and Brie Baguette

MAKES LUNCH FOR 2

This is a lot to heap on a slice of baguette—you can turn it into a sandwich by adding a top slice of bread.

INGREDIENTS

- 1 (6-in/15-cm) piece baguette, or 1 demi-baguette, halved horizontally
- 1 tablespoon Dijon mustard, or 2 tablespoons grainy mustard
- 1 cup (35 g) baby watercress
- 3 ounces (85 g) sliced roasted deli turkey
- 3 ounces (85 g) sliced Brie cheese
- ½ sweet apple, such as Fuji or Pink Lady, thinly sliced
  Flaky sea salt and freshly ground black pepper

HOW TO MAKE IT

Spread the cut side of both baguette pieces with the mustard. Top with the watercress, turkey, cheese, and apple. Sprinkle with salt and a few grinds of pepper. Eat right away.

Tangy Chicken Salad Tartine

MAKES LUNCH FOR 2

The chicken salad keeps well— you can whip this up for lunches two days in a row or share with a loved one.

INGREDIENTS

- 1 cup (5 oz/140 g) rotisserie chicken, shredded
- ½ cup (70 g) chopped roasted peppers
- 1 ounce (28 g) grated Cheddar cheese (¼ cup)
- 2 tablespoons chopped Lightly Pickled Cucumbers (page 224), or store-bought pickles
- 3 tablespoons Dijon mustard
- 2 tablespoons mayonnaise
- 1 tablespoon chopped fresh flat-leaf parsley leaves, plus more for serving

  Kosher salt and freshly ground black pepper
- 2 large slices olive bread, toasted

HOW TO MAKE IT

Mix the chicken, roasted peppers, Cheddar, pickles, mustard, mayonnaise, parsley, ½ teaspoon salt, and ¼ teaspoon pepper in a medium bowl. Spoon onto the toasted bread and sprinkle with more parsley. Eat right away.

Note: The chicken salad mixture can be made up to 2 days in advance. Store in an airtight container in the refrigerator.

Hard-Cooked Egg and Pimiento Cheese Tartine

MAKES LUNCH FOR 1

This toast hits all the egg-salad notes without being too mushy.

INGREDIENTS

- 1 large egg
- 1 large piece whole-grain bread, toasted
- 3 tablespoons pimiento cheese
- ¼ cup (35 g) cherry tomatoes, halved
- 1 teaspoon olive oil
- 2 teaspoons chopped fresh chives

  Flaky sea salt, freshly ground black pepper, and lemon wedge, for serving

HOW TO MAKE IT

Bring a small pot of water to a boil. Using a long-handled spoon, gently lower the egg into the water. Roughly dropping it in can cause the shell to crack on the bottom of the pot.

Turn the heat down to a gentle simmer and set a timer for 9 minutes. Carefully remove the cooked egg and submerge in an ice bath or run under cold water until cool enough to handle. Tap the egg gently on the counter and roll to crack the shell all over. Peel the shell off and then slice the egg crosswise into 4 slices.

Spread the pimiento cheese on the toast. Nestle the tomatoes and eggs in the pimiento cheese, then drizzle with the oil and sprinkle with the chives, some flaky sea salt, and a few grinds of pepper. Squeeze the lemon wedge over the top and eat right away.

Prosciutto and Cucumber Tartine

MAKES LUNCH FOR 1

Have you ever had a butter and cucumber English tea sandwich? Those ones with the crusts cut off, that sound like they'd be gross, but are actually delicious. Here, I add a lemony herb butter for bright, complex flavor and a slice of prosciutto for richness (and elegance)—altogether a deeply satisfying midday meal.

INGREDIENTS

- 1 tablespoon Lemony Parsley Butter (page 227)
- 1 slice sourdough bread, preferably whole wheat, toasted
- ¼ cup (2 oz/55 g) thinly sliced cucumber
- 1 ounce (28 g) thinly sliced prosciutto

  Lemon wedge and freshly ground black pepper, for serving

HOW TO MAKE IT

Spread the Lemony Parsley Butter on the bread, then top with the cucumber slices, pressing to help them settle into the butter. Top with the prosciutto and then squeeze the lemon wedge over the top. Sprinkle with a grind or two of pepper and eat right away.

No-Cook Lunches

When you've got leftovers in the fridge, you've got lunch. But, what if you hate leftovers, or if you don't have any on hand? This is where no-cook lunches come into play. It can be as simple as tucking vegetables in hummus into a pita (page 91) or assembling a plate of snacks like a grown-up Lunchable (page 95). These all come together quickly and make one or two servings.

Hummus and Veggie Pita

MAKES LUNCH FOR 1

You can add protein with a sliced, hard-cooked egg or two. Lay the slices in a single layer on top of the hummus before adding the tomato salad. I like plain hummus best here because it allows you to control flavor, but use whatever kind you like. Garlic and roasted red pepper would be particularly delicious.

INGREDIENTS

- 1 small tomato, chopped (about ¾ cup/135 g)
- 1 small carrot, grated (about ¼ cup/30 g)
- 2 tablespoons chopped pickled banana peppers, spicy or mild
- 1 ounce (28 g) crumbled feta cheese

  A generous handful fresh cilantro leaves

  Kosher salt and freshly ground black pepper
- 1 whole-wheat pita, split and toasted
- ¼ cup (60 g) plain hummus

  Olive oil, for drizzling

HOW TO MAKE IT

In a small bowl, toss together the tomato, carrot, pickled banana peppers, cheese, cilantro, and ¼ teaspoon each salt and pepper. This can be done up to 6 hours in advance.

Just before serving, spread the inside of the pita with the hummus, then pile the tomato salad into the pocket. Drizzle with a bit of oil and sprinkle with additional salt and pepper.

Pesto Chicken Caprese

MAKES LUNCH FOR 1 OR 2

This lunch is protein-packed and sits well at room temperature for a couple hours. If it'll be any longer than that, refrigerate until 30 minutes before you eat. If you want to add volume and some more fiber, serve this over a bed of romaine or baby arugula.

INGREDIENTS

- 1 cup (5 oz/140 g) shredded rotisserie chicken
- 1 tablespoon pesto
- 1 cup (145 g) halved cherry tomatoes
- ½ cup halved bocconcini (small mozzarella balls)

  Kosher salt and freshly ground black pepper

HOW TO MAKE IT

Toss the chicken with the pesto in a small bowl so it's evenly coated. Fold in the tomatoes, mozzarella, ½ teaspoon salt, and ¼ teaspoon pepper.

Greek Salad with Roast Beef

MAKES LUNCH FOR 1

When I have leftover steak, my go-to is a steak salad. When I don't have steak and the craving hits, I sub in roast beef for something just as delicious.

INGREDIENTS

- 3 ounces (85 g) roast beef
- 1 cup (105 g) chopped seedless cucumber
- 2 small tomatoes, cut into quarters
- ½ cup (30 g) sugar snap peas
- 2 tablespoons halved, pitted Kalamata olives
- 2 tablespoons crumbled feta cheese
- 2 tablespoons Dried Oregano Italian Vinaigrette (page 229)

  Flaky sea salt and freshly ground black pepper
- ½ romaine heart, sliced crosswise into ½-inch-thick (12-mm) ribbons

HOW TO MAKE IT

Mix the roast beef, cucumber, tomatoes, snap peas, olives, cheese, dressing, and ¼ teaspoon each salt and pepper in a small bowl. Fold in the romaine just before serving.

Take it to work: Mix everything except the romaine and transfer to a tall, wide-mouth jar or container. Top with the romaine and keep upright until serving—this ensures the lettuce doesn't get soggy.

Old-School Pizzeria Salad

MAKES A GENEROUS LUNCH FOR 1

I created this dish thinking about the flavors of a classic muffaletta salad. But, when it came down to tasting the final recipe, I realized I had created exactly the salad my family got alongside our pizzas growing up. I'm so glad to have it back.

INGREDIENTS

- ¾ cup (115 g) canned chickpeas, rinsed
- ⅔ cup (85 g) chopped giardiniera pickles
- ⅓ cup (1½ oz/40 g) Provolone cheese, cut into ½-inch (12-mm) cubes
- ⅓ cup (1½ oz/40 g) sliced salami, cut into ½-inch (12-mm) pieces
- 2 tablespoons Dried Oregano Italian Vinaigrette (page 229)

  Flaky sea salt and freshly ground black pepper
- 2 cups (40 g) baby arugula

HOW TO MAKE IT

Mix the chickpeas, giardiniera pickles, cheese, salami, dressing, and ¼ teaspoon each salt and pepper in a salad bowl. Fold in the arugula just before serving.

Take it to work: Mix everything except the arugula and transfer to a tall, skinny jar or container. Top with the arugula and keep upright until serving—this ensures the arugula doesn't get soggy.

Old-School
Pizzeria Salad

The All-Day Snacker

MAKES LUNCH FOR 1

If you're someone who prefers to snack throughout the day instead of eat three (or four) square meals, then this is for you. I like to think of it as a grownup Lunchable.

INGREDIENTS

- ½ avocado, pitted
- 2 ounces (55 g) Cheddar cheese, cut into cubes
- ¼ cup (35 g) roasted, salted marcona or regular almonds
- 1 large carrot, cut into matchsticks
- ¼ cup (40 g) mixed olives
- 2 Persian cucumbers, stemmed and cut into quarters lengthwise
- 2 ounces (55 g) seeded crackers, such as Mary's Gone Crackers or Ak-Mak

HOW TO MAKE IT

Lay a slice of plastic wrap directly on the surface of the avocado if you're packing your lunch in advance. Arrange all the ingredients in a container or on a plate, and eat as you like.

Summer Barley Bowl with Chorizo, Cucumbers, and Corn

MAKES LUNCH FOR 2

I give bonus points to any grain bowl that can last a long while in the fridge, and this one even improves in flavor as it sits. The cucumbers, radishes, and corn round out the intensity of the chorizo and salty feta. When you're ready to eat, make sure it comes to room temperature so all those delicious ingredients can shine through. This makes a great side salad for a dinner party, or make it a filling dinner by adding seared salmon fillets. Get easy instructions from Seared Salmon with Sautéed Squash and Greens (page 187).

INGREDIENTS

- 1½ cups (235 g) cooked pearl barley (page 236)

- 1 cup (145 g) raw corn kernels from 1 cob (see tip on page 242)

- 1 Persian cucumber, thinly sliced (about 1 cup/105 g)

- ½ cup chopped Lightly Pickled Cucumbers (page 224), or store-bought, plus 1 tablespoon liquid from the jar

- 3 or 4 radishes, thinly sliced (about ½ cup/60 g)

- 2 ounces (55 g) feta cheese, crumbled

- 1½ ounces (42 g) dried chorizo, about a 2-inch (5-cm) piece, thinly sliced

- 2 tablespoons olive oil

  Kosher salt and freshly ground black pepper

HOW TO MAKE IT

Toss the barley, corn, cucumber, pickles, radishes, cheese, chorizo, oil, and 1½ teaspoons each salt and pepper in a medium bowl.

Divide the salad between two containers and refrigerate until 1 hour before serving. Transfer to a bowl (or eat straight from the container) and let everything come to room temperature before eating.

→
**Miso Chicken
Noodle Soup**
PAGE 114

As a recipe developer, I ask anyone I meet what they need help cooking. Surprisingly often, the answer is soup. Across all cultures, soup holds a place in most people's hearts as something soul-warming and satisfying, but it turns out that many cooks find the prospect daunting.

Thankfully, soups are easier to make than you might fear. However, to make a flavorful soup, you *will* need a bit of time. This means that the recipes in this chapter take longer than other *Healthyish* ones, but a big batch of soup can last throughout the week or stock your freezer.

I use homemade chicken stock in all my recipes because I like the extra flavor and body that it adds. But high-quality store-bought works just as well, or use the Vegetable Stock on page 239 if you're vegetarian.

Cool any leftovers completely before transferring to single-serving containers. I like glass jars because I can stick them straight in the microwave to reheat, but pint containers stack very well in the freezer.

Sausage, Potato, White Bean, and Kale Soup

MAKES 12 CUPS; 4 TO 6 SERVINGS

A little bit of Italian sausage goes a long way in this hearty soup. Searing it at the beginning allows the rich flavor to permeate the entire soup as it cooks. Of course, if you want this to be vegetarian, skip the sausage and add an extra two tablespoons of olive oil when you cook the onion. If your grocery store doesn't sell loose sausage, you can easily take the casing off links. Using the tip of your knife, make a shallow cut lengthwise on one side of each sausage. Peel the casing off and discard.

INGREDIENTS

- 2 tablespoons olive oil
- 8 ounces (225 g) loose Italian sausage
- 2 onions (12 oz/340 g), chopped (about 2 cups)
- 1 teaspoon dried oregano
- 1 teaspoon fennel seeds
  Kosher salt and freshly ground black pepper
- 2 Yukon Gold potatoes (1 lb/455 g), cut into 1-inch (2.5-cm) pieces
- 8 cups (2 L) chicken stock from Whole Poached Chicken (page 241), or Vegetable Stock (page 239)
- 1 bay leaf (optional)
- 1 (15.5-oz/439-g) can cannellini beans, rinsed
- 1 large bunch kale (about 1 lb/455g), stemmed and leaves torn
- 2 tablespoons red wine vinegar
  Grated Parmesan cheese, for serving

HOW TO MAKE IT

Heat the oil in a large pot over medium-high heat. Add the sausage and break it up with a wooden spoon so it's in small, bite-size pieces. Don't touch the pieces for 2 to 3 minutes, until golden brown on the bottom. Using tongs, flip the sausage pieces over and leave them until cooked through and golden brown on all sides, 2 to 3 minutes more.

Transfer the sausage to a paper towel–lined plate, leaving the fat and oil behind in the pan. Cover the sausage with aluminum foil to keep in any moisture and set aside.

Return the pot to medium heat and add the onions, oregano, fennel seeds, 2 teaspoons salt, and 1 teaspoon pepper. Cook, stirring often, until the onions are translucent and soft, 10 to 12 minutes. Add the potatoes, stock, and bay leaf (if using). Cover and bring to a boil over high heat, then reduce to a gentle simmer and cook until the potatoes are fork-tender, 8 to 10 minutes.

Stir in the beans, kale, and reserved sausage. Cook until the beans are heated through. Fish out the bay leaf, stir in the vinegar, and taste and adjust the seasoning with more salt and pepper if you want.

Serve the soup hot with a pile of freshly grated cheese on top.

Curried Sweet Potato Soup

MAKES 12 CUPS; SERVES 4 TO 6

I can eat my fair share of steamed and roasted sweet potatoes, but the flavor can sometimes overpower savory preparations. In this soup, a hefty dose of curry powder tames that sweetness, transforming the flavor into something complex, hearty, and satisfying. Pumpkin seed oil has a lovely toasted nutty flavor, but a drizzle of olive oil tastes great, too.

INGREDIENTS

- ¼ cup (60 ml) olive oil
- 2 onions (12 oz/340 g), chopped (about 2 cups)
- Kosher salt and freshly ground black pepper
- 4 garlic cloves, chopped
- 2 teaspoons curry powder
- 1 teaspoon ground coriander
- 8 cups (2 L) chicken stock from Whole Poached Chicken (page 241), or Vegetable Stock (page 239)
- 3 large sweet potatoes (3 lbs/ 1.4 kg), cut into ¾-inch (2-cm) pieces
- 2 large carrots, chopped
- 1 tablespoon fresh lime juice
- Fresh cilantro leaves, toasted pumpkin seeds, and pumpkin seed oil, for serving

HOW TO MAKE IT

Heat the oil in a large pot over medium heat. Add the onions, 2 teaspoons salt, and 1 teaspoon pepper. Cook, stirring often, until the onions are translucent and soft, 10 to 12 minutes. Stir in the garlic, curry powder, and coriander and cook until the garlic is fragrant, about 1 minute more.

Add the stock, sweet potatoes, and carrots to the pot, cover, and bring to a boil over high heat. Reduce to a strong simmer and cook, stirring here and there, until the sweet potatoes are very soft, 25 to 30 minutes.

Purée the soup, using a blender in batches or a handheld immersion blender. Stir in the lime juice and ½ teaspoon salt.

Serve the soup topped with cilantro, toasted pumpkin seeds, and a drizzle of pumpkin seed oil.

Summer Corn Soup

MAKES 12 CUPS; SERVES 4 TO 6

If you've ever enjoyed Mexican street corn—spread with cheese and chili pepper—then you also know the frustrations of picking corn out of your teeth. This has all those flavors, but in a more convenient package. You can eat this soup hot off the stove, or chill it in the refrigerator for a cooling lunch or dinner on a steamy summer day.

INGREDIENTS

¼ cup (½ stick) unsalted butter

2 onions (12 oz/340 g), chopped (about 2 cups)

Kosher salt and freshly ground black pepper

2 garlic cloves, chopped

2 teaspoons ground cumin

2 teaspoons chili powder

8 cups (1.2 kg) corn kernels from 8 cobs (see tip on page 242) or the same amount frozen

2 russet potatoes (about 2 lbs/ 910 g), peeled and cut into ¾-inch (2-cm) pieces

8 cups (2 L) chicken stock from Whole Poached Chicken (page 241), or Vegetable Stock (page 239)

3 tablespoons fresh lime juice

4 ounces (115 g) Cotija cheese, crumbled

Fresh cilantro leaves, for serving

HOW TO MAKE IT

Heat the butter in a large pot over medium heat. Add the onions, 2 teaspoons salt, and 1 teaspoon pepper. Cook, stirring often, until the onions are translucent and soft, 10 to 12 minutes. Add the garlic, cumin, and chili powder and cook until fragrant, 30 seconds to 1 minute more.

Reserve ½ cup of the corn kernels to use as garnish and set aside. Stir in the remaining 7½ cups corn, the potatoes, and stock, cover, and bring to a boil. Reduce to a strong simmer. Cook, stirring here and there, until the potatoes are completely soft, 15 to 18 minutes.

Purée the soup, using a blender in batches or a handheld immersion blender. Stir in the lime juice and ½ teaspoon salt.

Serve the soup topped with cheese, cilantro, reserved corn kernels, and a few grinds pepper.

Loaded Baked Potato and Cauliflower Soup

MAKES 12 CUPS; SERVES 4 TO 6

True or false? The best part of a baked potato is the toppings. If you agree, then this soup is perfect for you. Starting off with bacon fat means that the entire soup is infused with delicious, smoky flavor. And, instead of just using starch-heavy potatoes, a blend of potato and cauliflower makes for a creamier, lighter soup. All this as balance for the classic baked potato toppings, naturally.

INGREDIENTS

- 4 large slices (8 oz/225 g) extra-thick cut bacon
- 2 onions (12 oz/340 g), chopped (about 2 cups)

  Kosher salt and freshly ground black pepper

- 2 large russet potatoes (2 lbs/ 910 g), peeled and cut into ½-inch (12-mm) pieces (about 5 cups)
- 1 medium head cauliflower (1¼ lbs/570 g), cut into small florets (about 6 cups)
- 8 cups (2 L) chicken stock from Whole Poached Chicken (page 241), or Vegetable Stock (page 239)

  Sour cream, chopped fresh chives, and grated Cheddar cheese, for serving

HOW TO MAKE IT

Heat a large soup pot over medium-low heat. Place the bacon slices flat in the pot and cook, turning a couple times, until crispy and most of the fat has drained from the bacon, 8 to 12 minutes total. Using tongs, transfer the bacon to a paper towel–lined plate, leaving the fat in the pot.

Add the onions, 2 teaspoons salt, and 1 teaspoon pepper. Cook, stirring often, until the onions are translucent and soft, 10 to 12 minutes.

Stir in the potatoes, cauliflower, and stock, cover, and bring to a boil over high heat. Reduce to a strong simmer and cook, stirring here and there, until the potatoes are very soft, 15 to 20 minutes.

Purée the soup, using a blender in batches or a handheld immersion blender. Taste and season with additional salt and pepper, if you like.

Slice or tear the cooked bacon into bite-size pieces and sprinkle it over bowls of the soup. Serve topped with sour cream, chives, and cheese.

Red Lentil Soup with Cilantro-Lime Yogurt

MAKES 10 CUPS; SERVES 4 TO 6

At its core, this soup is just olive oil, vegetables, lentils, and some spices, but add in the elements of heat and time and you've got something immensely comforting and soothing. Sometimes there can be dirt or tiny stones mixed in with lentils, so pick through and rinse them well before adding to the pot.

INGREDIENTS

- ¼ cup (60 ml) plus 2 tablespoons olive oil
- 2 onions (12 oz/340 g), chopped (about 2 cups)
- 5 medium carrots, chopped small
- 5 celery stalks, chopped small
- 1 teaspoon ground ginger

  Kosher salt and freshly ground black pepper
- 8 cups (2 L) chicken stock from Whole Poached Chicken (page 241), or Vegetable Stock (page 239)
- 1 pound (455 g) red lentils (2½ scant cups), well rinsed
- 2 tablespoons yellow mustard seeds
- ⅔ cup (165 ml) plain Greek yogurt
- ¼ cup chopped fresh cilantro leaves
- 2 tablespoons fresh lime juice

HOW TO MAKE IT

Heat ¼ cup (60 ml) of the oil in a large pot over medium heat. Add the onions, carrots, celery, ground ginger, 1 tablespoon salt, and 1 teaspoon pepper and cook, stirring often, until the vegetables are very soft, 18 to 20 minutes. Stir in the stock, lentils, and mustard seeds. Cover, and bring to a boil over high heat. Reduce to a simmer and cook until the lentils are totally soft and falling apart, about 15 minutes more.

Purée the soup, using a blender in batches or a handheld immersion blender.

In a small bowl, stir together the yogurt, cilantro, lime juice, remaining 2 tablespoons olive oil, and ½ teaspoon each salt and pepper.

Serve the soup with a dollop of the yogurt and more salt and pepper, if you like.

Pozole with Pinto Beans and Queso Fresco

MAKES 14 CUPS; SERVES 4 TO 6

I rarely play favorites, but this is in my top five *Healthyish* recipes. Pozole is a traditional Mexican soup made with hominy—dried corn kernels—and a rich broth. Instead of the classic pork, I use chicken here for a lighter take. If you've already made the Whole Poached Chicken (page 241), or use rotisserie chicken and store-bought stock, this will come together quickly.

INGREDIENTS

- 2 tablespoons vegetable or canola oil
- 2 teaspoons chili powder

  Kosher salt and freshly ground black pepper
- 6 medium or 8 small tomatillos (1 lb/455 g), halved
- 3 poblano peppers (12 oz/340 g), quartered and seeded
- 1 medium yellow onion, quartered and leaves pulled apart
- 4 garlic cloves, peeled
- 4 cups (775 g) shredded chicken and 8 cups (2 L) chicken stock from Whole Poached Chicken (page 241)
- 1 (29-oz/822-g) can hominy, rinsed
- 1 (15.5-oz/439-g) can pinto beans, rinsed
- 1 tablespoon fresh lime juice, plus wedges for serving
- 1 teaspoon granulated sugar

  Crumbled queso fresco cheese, sliced radishes, fresh cilantro leaves, and Quick-Pickled Red Onions (page 222), for serving

HOW TO MAKE IT

Turn your broiler to high and set a rack as close as possible to the heat source while still able to fit the baking sheet between the rack and the broiler.

Mix the oil, chili powder, 2 teaspoons salt, and 1 teaspoon pepper in a small bowl. Put the tomatillos, poblano peppers, onion, and garlic on an aluminum foil–lined rimmed baking sheet and rub all over with the oil–chili powder mixture. Broil, tossing once, until everything is golden brown and can be easily pierced with a fork, 13 to 15 minutes. It's OK if there's some char on the vegetables.

Transfer the contents of the baking sheet to a blender and purée until completely smooth. Pour into a large soup pot and add the stock. Cover and bring to a boil over high heat. Reduce the heat to a simmer and add the chicken, hominy, and beans. Cook until everything is heated through, 5 to 7 minutes more. Stir in the lime juice, sugar, 1 teaspoon salt, and ¼ teaspoon pepper.

Serve topped with the cheese, radishes, cilantro, pickled red onions, and lime wedges.

Cheesy Broccoli and Pea Soup

MAKES 12 CUPS; SERVES 4 TO 6

There's something about the combination of toasted caraway and rich, salty Parmesan that makes this soup taste supremely hearty.

INGREDIENTS

- 3 tablespoons olive oil
- 2 onions (12 oz/340 g), chopped (about 2 cups)
- 1 teaspoon caraway seeds, crushed
- Kosher salt and freshly ground black pepper
- 3 (10-oz/280-g) bags frozen broccoli florets (about 9 cups)
- 6 cups (1.4 L) chicken stock from Whole Poached Chicken (page 241), or Vegetable Stock (page 239)
- 2 ounces finely grated Parmesan cheese (about ½ cup packed/ 55 g), plus the rind
- 1 (10-oz/280-g) bag frozen peas (about 2 cups)
- 2 tablespoons lemon juice
- Buttered crusty toast, for serving

HOW TO MAKE IT

Heat the oil in a large pot over medium-high heat. Add the onions, caraway seeds, 2 teaspoons salt, and ½ teaspoon pepper. Cook, stirring often, until the onions are golden and translucent, 10 to 12 minutes.

Add the broccoli, stock, and Parmesan rind and stir so that the broccoli is almost entirely submerged beneath the stock. Cover and bring to a boil, then reduce to a simmer. Cook until the broccoli is very tender, 9 to 12 minutes. Add the peas and stir until they're heated through, about 1 minute more.

Remove the Parmesan rind. Puree the soup, using a blender in batches or a handheld immersion blender. Stir in the lemon juice and 1 teaspoon salt.

Serve the soup topped with the grated Parmesan, salt and pepper, and a buttered slice of crusty toast.

Miso Chicken Noodle Soup

MAKES 10 CUPS; SERVES 4 TO 6

When I was growing up, my mom made a version of this quick soup, which she finished by dropping an egg yolk right into the hot broth. It breaks open and creates a deliciously creamy sauce. I do the same here, but if you're squeamish about the yolk, feel free to skip it.

INGREDIENTS

- 2 cups (390 g) chicken and 8 cups (2 L) chicken stock from Whole Poached Chicken (page 241)
- 3 tablespoons white miso paste
- ¼ cup (60 ml) soy sauce
- 1 bunch scallions, very thinly sliced, some green parts saved for serving
- 1 (14-oz/400-g) package extra-firm tofu, cut into ½-inch (12-mm) cubes
- 8 ounces (225 g) udon or soba noodles
- 4 to 6 large egg yolks
- 1 cup (150 g) kimchi

HOW TO MAKE IT

Bring the chicken stock to a boil in a covered large pot over high heat.

In a small bowl, whisk the miso and 1 tablespoon of the soy sauce. (You do this so that the miso can easily integrate with the stock, otherwise you'll get big clumps.) Add this to the pot with the remaining 3 tablespoons soy sauce, the scallions, and tofu.

Return to a boil and add the noodles. Cook until they're just barely tender, 2 to 3 minutes, then stir in the chicken and cook until the noodles are al dente and the chicken is hot, 2 to 3 minutes more. Ladle the soup into bowls while it's super hot and then drop an egg yolk into each bowl. Stir to mix the yolk into the soup, and then top with the kimchi and more scallion greens.

→
**One-Pot
Whole-Wheat
Spring Pasta**
PAGE 126

CHAPTER 5

Vegetarian Dinners

Every time I create a vegetarian recipe, I ask myself, "Would my dad love this?" His gut reaction to meat-free meals is "Not for me," so I know it's a home run when he cleans his plate without asking where the chicken is. These all pass the Dad test, with flying colors.

EGG-BASED RECIPES

If you've been eating vegetarian for a long time, then you're accustomed to eating eggs for dinner. Cut to the recent "Put an Egg on It" craze, and it doesn't seem too wild to top savory polenta and beans with a crispy fried egg. These satisfying moments are what allow eggs to feel like a hearty dinner. These recipes are larger quantities than the breakfast eggs and the cooking time is longer.

PASTA AND OTHER WHEAT-BASED CARBS

With *Healthyish* eating, as with many things in life, moderation is key. Cutting out pasta full-stop can feel restrictive, and lead to a binge. (Hey, we've all been there.) Instead, I like to bulk up pasta with vegetables. For instance, trumpet mushrooms play the role of sea scallops on page 128. The Roasted Vegetable and Barley Bowls (page 135) and Kimchi-Fried Farro (page 125) call for wheat-based whole grains, but if you're gluten-free, swap quinoa or brown rice.

GLUTEN-FREE, EGG-FREE RECIPES

Fear not, gluten- and egg-free doesn't mean flavor-free. In fact, these are three of my favorite recipes in the book. Roasting chickpeas gives a satisfying heft to a roasted vegetable salad, curry powder powerfully transforms cauliflower in a kale Caesar, and a tangy slaw upgrades a rice-and-bean bowl.

Smoky Cauliflower and Onion Frittata

MAKES DINNER FOR 4 TO 6

Starting the cauliflower and onions together in water is unconventional, but it allows the veg to steam through and finish with a little browning. The wide skillet also allows you to cook the veg in the same pan that you make the frittata in, but it means the frittata comes out on the thinner side. If you like a thick wedge, transfer the cooked cauliflower and onions to a 9-inch (23-cm) skillet, but keep in mind this will make the baking time longer. Extra frittata is your breakfast ace-in-the-hole. Heat leftovers in the microwave or toaster oven and serve between a soft, toasted bun with a heap of greens and a schmear of Dijon mustard and mayo.

INGREDIENTS

- 2 tablespoons olive oil
- 1 medium cauliflower (about 1¾ lbs/ 800 g), cut into the smallest florets you can manage
- 1 large or 2 medium onions, thinly sliced
- ¼ cup (60 ml) water
- 2 teaspoons smoked paprika
- Kosher salt and freshly ground black pepper
- 9 large eggs
- ¼ cup (60 ml) whole milk
- 3 ounces Gruyère cheese, grated (about ¾ cup/80 g)
- 2 tablespoons chopped fresh flat-leaf parsley
- 5 ounces (140 g) mixed greens (about 6 cups)
- Cidery Dijon Vinaigrette (page 233)

HOW TO MAKE IT

Preheat your oven to 425°F (220°C), with a rack positioned in the center of the oven.

Heat the oil in an ovenproof, large skillet over medium-high heat. (I like a 10-inch/25-cm, straight-sided sauté pan.) Add the cauliflower, onions, water, paprika, 2 teaspoons salt, and 1 teaspoon pepper and stir to distribute. Cover, and cook, stirring often, until the onions are soft and you can easily pierce the cauliflower with a fork, 14 to 18 minutes. If the liquid hasn't evaporated, cook uncovered for a couple minutes more.

Whisk the eggs, milk, 1½ teaspoons salt, and ¼ teaspoon pepper in a medium bowl. Stir in the cheese and parsley until evenly distributed. Pour the egg mixture over the onions and cauliflower. Carefully transfer the skillet to the oven and bake for 15 to 20 minutes, until the frittata is set but still barely jiggles in the center.

Remove the frittata from the oven and let it sit for 10 minutes. Toss the greens and vinaigrette in a salad bowl. Serve the frittata with the salad.

Polenta Rounds with Fried Eggs and Avocado-Bean Salsa

MAKES DINNER FOR 4

Using precooked polenta is a great time-saving shortcut. Not to mention, I find bubbling polenta to be a huge mess and I'm always scared the splatters will burn me. You can find logs of cooked polenta right next to the uncooked polenta at your grocery store. If you can't find it, or would rather cook it yourself, just prepare instant or regular polenta according to package directions.

INGREDIENTS

- 1 (15.5-oz/439-g) can pinto beans, rinsed
- 1 avocado, chopped
- ¼ cup fresh cilantro leaves, plus more for serving
- ¼ cup Quick-Pickled Red Onions (page 222)
- 2 tablespoons olive oil, plus more if needed
- 1 tablespoon red wine vinegar

    Kosher salt and freshly ground black pepper

- 8 (¾-inch-thick/2-cm) slices cooked polenta rounds
- 4 large eggs

HOW TO MAKE IT

Toss the beans, avocado, cilantro, onions, 1 tablespoon of the oil, the vinegar, and ¾ teaspoon each salt and pepper in a small bowl. Set aside while you cook the polenta and eggs.

Heat the remaining 1 tablespoon oil in a large nonstick skillet over medium-high heat. Add the rounds of polenta and season with a little salt and pepper. Cook until golden brown and crispy, 3 to 5 minutes per side. (You can do this in two batches if you don't have a large enough skillet.) Transfer the polenta to a plate, cover with aluminum foil to keep warm, and set aside.

There should be oil left in the skillet you cooked the polenta in, but if there's not, add a bit more. Add the eggs to the skillet, cover, and cook until the edges are crispy and the yolk and whites are set, 2 to 3 minutes. Season with salt and pepper to taste.

Top the polenta with the eggs and avocado-bean salsa. Sprinkle with a little salt and pepper, more cilantro leaves, and serve.

Shortcut Shakshuka for Two

MAKES DINNER FOR 2

Shakshuka is a dish made from eggs poached in a tomato-onion sauce. I use ready-to-go marinara for a quick, flavorful shortcut. Spinach adds fiber and bulks up the salty sauce.

INGREDIENTS

- 1 tablespoon olive oil, plus more for drizzling
- 1 small onion, very thinly sliced
- 1 small garlic clove, sliced
- Kosher salt and freshly ground black pepper
- 1 cup (240 ml) marinara sauce
- ½ cup (120 ml) water
- 10 ounces (280 g) frozen spinach, chopped (about 2½ cups)
- 4 large eggs
- 2 ounces (55 g) feta cheese, crumbled
- Toasted crusty bread and chopped fresh flat-leaf parsley leaves, for serving

HOW TO MAKE IT

Heat the oil in a medium nonstick or cast-iron skillet over medium-high heat.

Add the onion, garlic, and ¼ teaspoon each salt and pepper. Cook, stirring here and there, until the onion is soft, 6 to 8 minutes.

Add the marinara sauce and water, cover, and cook until the marinara sauce is bubbling, 2 to 3 minutes. Stir in the spinach until it's coated with the sauce. Using your spatula, make wells in the spinach—one for each egg. Crack the eggs into the wells one at a time, then dot the pan all over with the crumbled cheese. Cover again and cook until the whites are set but the yolks still jiggle when you shake the pan a bit, 2 to 3 minutes.

Season with additional salt and pepper, if you like. Drizzle with olive oil, sprinkle with parsley, and serve with the bread.

Kimchi-Fried Farro

A MAKES DINNER FOR 2

An ex-boyfriend of mine bought tickets to a Korean cooking class a couple years ago. Huge win: we made kimchi–fried rice and it quickly became a go-to dinner. Here, I go heavy on the eggs (for protein) and toast up nutty farro for body. But, any grain will work well so if you've got something else on hand, use it!

INGREDIENTS

4   large eggs

Kosher salt and freshly ground black pepper

1   tablespoon vegetable oil

1½ cups (300 g) cooked farro (page 237)

1½ cups (225 g) chopped kimchi

½   cup (80 g) canned adzuki beans, rinsed

½   cup chopped fresh cilantro leaves, plus more for serving

1   avocado, sliced

HOW TO MAKE IT

Beat the eggs with 1 teaspoon salt and ¼ teaspoon pepper. Heat the oil in a medium nonstick skillet over medium-high heat. Add the farro and cook until golden brown, 4 to 6 minutes. Stir it only a few times so the farro toasts and crisps.

Add 1 cup of the kimchi and the beans and cook, stirring often, until hot, about 2 minutes more. Turn the heat down to low and pour in the eggs. Immediately start stirring with a spatula and cook until the eggs are cooked but still soft, about 1 minute. Stir in the cilantro.

Divide the farro between two bowls and top with the remaining ½ cup kimchi, the sliced avocado, and extra cilantro.

One-Pot Whole-Wheat Spring Pasta

MAKES DINNER FOR 4

Olive oil AND butter? How UN-healthy, you say. Well, not exactly. Sometimes butter is necessary for its richness, mouthfeel, and satiety. Whole-wheat pasta can taste like cardboard, so finishing with butter rounds out and mellows any unwanted earthiness. This is the same method as One-Pot Spicy and Creamy Chicken Pasta (page 157), so once you've mastered this method, you can make that one just as easily.

INGREDIENTS

- 1 tablespoon olive oil
- 2 large shallots (4 oz/115 g), thinly sliced (about 1 cup)

  Kosher salt and freshly ground black pepper
- 1 pound (455 g) asparagus, sliced diagonally into 1-inch (2.5-cm) pieces
- 12 ounces (340 g) short whole-wheat pasta (such as penne rigate, fusilli, or rigatoni)
- 3 cups (720 ml) water
- 1 cup (135 g) frozen peas
- 2 tablespoons fresh lemon juice, plus 1 teaspoon finely grated lemon zest
- 2 ounces finely grated Parmesan cheese (about ½ cup/55 g)
- 2 tablespoons unsalted butter
- 1 tablespoon chopped fresh tarragon leaves

HOW TO MAKE IT

Heat the oil in a large straight-sided sauté pan or large pot. Add the shallots, 1 teaspoon salt, and ½ teaspoon pepper. Cook, stirring often, until the shallots are starting to soften, 4 to 6 minutes. Add the asparagus, pasta, water, and peas. Cover and bring to a boil.

Reduce the heat to a gentle simmer and cook, stirring here and there, until the pasta is just tender, 11 to 14 minutes. Remove from the heat when there's still a little water left—you're looking for just enough to create a sauce. Stir in the lemon juice and zest, Parmesan, butter, and tarragon, and season with ½ teaspoon salt and ¼ teaspoon pepper. Serve hot.

Use a larger cutting board, mixing bowl, or colander than you think you need. You'll be happy to have the extra space!

Linguine with Trumpet Mushroom "Scallops"

MAKES DINNER FOR 4

Sautéed trumpet mushrooms look like scallops, but are much more forgiving to cook, and a hell of a lot cheaper. I love them in this pasta—it feels surprisingly elegant—but you could make the mushrooms on their own for salads or grain bowls. Most of the recipes in this book call for whole-wheat or whole-grain pasta, but I use white pasta here since whole wheat's earthy flavor can overwhelm the mushrooms.

INGREDIENTS

Kosher salt and freshly ground black pepper

12 ounces (340 g) linguine

¼ cup (60 ml) canola or vegetable oil

1 pound (455 g) trumpet mushrooms, cut into ¾-inch-thick (2-cm) rounds

¼ cup chopped fresh chives

2 tablespoons fresh lemon juice

1 tablespoon unsalted butter

HOW TO MAKE IT

Bring a large pot of water to a rolling boil. Salt aggressively and add the linguine. Cook until 3 minutes before the package says the pasta will be done. Use a liquid measuring cup to scoop out 1 cup (240 ml) of the pasta water, set the water aside, then drain the pasta.

Meanwhile, heat the oil in a large skillet over medium-high heat. Add the mushrooms and season with 1 teaspoon each salt and pepper. Cook the mushrooms, stirring a few times, until golden brown on both sides, 10 to 14 minutes. You want them to brown nicely, so avoid stirring too much.

Add the cooked pasta to the pan with ¾ cup (180 ml) of the reserved pasta water and cook, stirring constantly, until the pasta is cooked through, 1 to 3 minutes more. Add the remaining ¼ cup (60 ml) pasta water if the pasta is too dry.

Remove from the heat, stir in the chives, lemon juice, and butter, and season with 1 teaspoon salt and ¼ teaspoon pepper. Serve hot.

Saucy Butternut Squash and White Beans with Pesto Couscous

MAKES DINNER FOR 4

Honestly, sometimes butternut squash feels like more work than I've bargained for. It's a lot of effort to peel! I get it. So, if it makes YOUR life easier, splurge on the precut cubes. Yeah, they're more expensive than doing it yourself, but it's sometimes worth saving the time. The size of pre-cut squash varies, so you might need to cook the cubes longer before adding in the beans.

INGREDIENTS

- 2 tablespoons olive oil
- 2 onions (12 oz/340 g), chopped (about 2 cups)
- Kosher salt and freshly ground black pepper
- 1 small butternut squash (about 1¾ lbs/800 g), peeled and cut into ½-inch (12-mm) pieces
- ¼ teaspoon ground nutmeg
- 2 cups (480 ml) Vegetable Stock (page 239), or water
- 1 (15.5-oz/439-g) can white beans, such as cannellini or navy beans, rinsed
- 3 tablespoons fresh lemon juice
- 1½ cups (290 g) white or whole-wheat couscous
- 1½ cups (360 ml) boiling water
- ¼ cup (65 g) pesto, plus more for serving
- 1 avocado, sliced
- ¼ cup (25 g) sliced almonds, toasted

HOW TO MAKE IT

Heat the oil in a large pot over medium heat. Add the onion, 1½ teaspoons salt, and ½ teaspoon pepper. Cook, stirring often, until the onion is soft, 10 to 12 minutes. Add the squash, nutmeg, and stock (or water), cover, and bring to a boil. Reduce the heat to a gentle simmer and cook, stirring occasionally, until you can easily pierce a piece of the squash with a fork, 12 to 14 minutes. (The liquid should have thickened considerably.)

Stir in the beans and cook until they're heated through, about 3 minutes more. Stir in 2 tablespoons of the lemon juice and season with 1 teaspoon salt and ½ teaspoon pepper.

Put the couscous in a medium heatproof bowl. Pour the boiling water over and cover with plastic wrap. Set a timer for 5 minutes—the couscous is ready when there's no liquid left. Use a fork to fluff the grains, then fold in the pesto, the remaining 1 tablespoon lemon juice, and ½ teaspoon each salt and pepper.

Serve the squash on top of the couscous, topped with the avocado and almonds. Season with salt and pepper, if you like, and top with a dollop of pesto.

131

Crispy Broccoli, Pepper, and Burrata Sheet Pan Dinner

MAKES DINNER FOR 4

For this recipe, you're looking for a squishy loaf of bread that has a crackly crust. Anything too fancy or dense will not crisp up or brown nicely. And, it's key that your baking sheet is rimmed, otherwise everything might slide off into the oven.

INGREDIENTS

- 1½ pounds (680 g) broccoli florets, from 2 generous broccoli heads (about 9 cups)
- 2 large bell peppers (1 lb/455 g total), seeded and sliced ½ inch (12 mm) thick
- 1 (13.75-oz/390-g) can quartered artichoke hearts, drained
- 1 lemon, sliced
- 3 tablespoons olive oil
- Kosher salt and freshly ground black pepper
- 8 ounces (225 g) soft French bread, cut into 1-inch (2.5-cm) cubes
- 8 ounces (225 g) burrata or fresh mozzarella cheese
- ¼ cup (35 g) pine nuts, toasted
- ½ cup fresh basil leaves, torn if large

HOW TO MAKE IT

Preheat your oven to 425°F (220°C), with a rack positioned in the top of the oven.

Toss the broccoli, bell peppers, artichokes, lemon, 2 tablespoons of the oil, 1½ teaspoons salt, and 1 teaspoon pepper on a rimmed baking sheet. Roast, tossing once, until the broccoli and peppers are just tender, 20 to 24 minutes.

Toss the bread with the remaining 1 tablespoon oil and ¼ teaspoon each salt and pepper. Scatter the bread cubes evenly over the vegetables. Return the baking sheet to the oven and roast until the bread cubes are golden brown and crispy on the outside and the vegetables are fork-tender, 14 to 18 minutes more.

Using your hands, shred the burrata into bite-size pieces and scatter over the baking sheet. Sprinkle the pine nuts and basil over the top and season with additional salt and pepper, if you like. Serve immediately.

Roasted Vegetable and Barley Bowls

MAKES DINNER FOR 4

The base recipe for these bowls is simple and makes a filling meal in its own right. I've also included ways to add protein, texture, and new flavors. Once you've got the hang of the method, you can change up the vegetables, too.

INGREDIENTS

For the vegetables:

3 large beets (1 lb/455 g), peeled and cut into ½-inch (12-mm) wedges

5 large carrots (about 1 lb/455 g), cut diagonally into ¾-inch (2-cm) pieces

1 pound (455 g) green beans, stems trimmed

3 tablespoons canola or vegetable oil

5 garlic cloves

3 fresh rosemary sprigs

2 teaspoons dried oregano

   Kosher salt and freshly ground black pepper

For the bowls:

5 ounces (140 g) tender lettuce, such as red leaf, butter lettuce, or Bibb (about 5 cups)

3 cups (470 g) cooked pearl barley (page 237)

4 ounces (115 g) fresh goat cheese, crumbled

⅓ cup Cidery Dijon Vinaigrette (page 233)

HOW TO MAKE IT

Preheat your oven to 425°F (220°C), with racks positioned in the top and bottom thirds of the oven.

Toss the beets, carrots, and beans with the oil, garlic, rosemary, oregano, 2 teaspoons salt, and 1 teaspoon pepper in a large bowl. Divide between two rimmed baking sheets and roast, tossing once, until you can easily pierce a beet with a fork, 25 to 30 minutes.

To serve, layer the lettuce, barley, vegetables, and cheese in large, shallow bowls, dividing them equally. Drizzle with the vinaigrette and season with additional salt and pepper.

More protein: add avocado, shredded chicken, tuna, or a hard-boiled egg

Extra texture: add green olives, poppy seeds, toasted nuts, or sesame seeds

Switch up the flavors: skip the herbs and roast with 1 teaspoon cumin and 1 teaspoon coriander OR 1 teaspoon smoked paprika and 1 teaspoon oregano.

Kale Caesar with Curried Cauliflower

MAKES DINNER FOR 4

This is an unusual combination of ingredients, but trust me, the salty-rich dressing, spicy cauliflower, and crunchy kale balance each other perfectly. Kale can handle many hours with dressing on it without wilting too much. So, if you want to make this ahead, go all the way through the recipe, but don't add the avocado until you're ready to eat.

INGREDIENTS

- 1 large bunch kale (about 1 lb/455g), stemmed and leaves torn
- 2 tablespoons plus 1 teaspoon olive oil

  Kosher salt and freshly ground black pepper
- 2 garlic cloves, crushed
- 1 medium head cauliflower, cut into small florets (about 7 cups/930 g prepared)
- 2 teaspoons curry powder
- 1 teaspoon crushed red pepper flakes
- ⅓ cup (75 ml) water
- ⅓ to ½ cup Eggless Caesar Dressing (page 232), depending on how rich you like your salad
- 2 avocados, chopped
- ½ cup (45 g) quartered Peppadews (about 10), or any pickled pepper
- ¼ cup toasted sliced almonds

HOW TO MAKE IT

Using your hands, massage the kale leaves with 1 teaspoon of the oil and ¼ teaspoon salt in a large bowl. This will help tenderize the leaves so they don't taste so garden-y.

Heat the remaining 2 tablespoons oil in a large skillet over medium heat. Add the garlic and cook until fragrant, 30 seconds to 1 minute. Use a slotted spoon to discard the garlic. (Or eat it smashed on oiled toast.)

Add the cauliflower, curry powder, red pepper flakes, and 1 teaspoon salt to the skillet. Stir in the water, cover, and cook over medium-high heat, stirring here and there, until the cauliflower is golden brown and you can easily insert a fork into a piece, 6 to 8 minutes. The water should have evaporated. Remove from the heat and let cool for 10 minutes.

To serve, toss the kale with the dressing and then fold in the cauliflower, avocados, peppadews, and almonds. Season to taste with additional salt and pepper.

Spiced Chickpea, Carrot, and Delicata Squash Salad

MAKES DINNER FOR 4

This is one of the few salads that I feel comfortable calling dinner. Delicata squash and carrots have a meaty texture to them when roasted, and the chickpeas add welcome crunch. Blue cheese can be polarizing, so if it's too funky for you, try goat cheese.

INGREDIENTS

- ¼ cup (60 ml) olive oil
- 2 teaspoons ground cumin
- 1 teaspoon ground coriander
- Kosher salt and freshly ground black pepper
- 2 delicata squash (2 to 2½ lbs/910 g to 1.2 kg), sliced into ½-inch (12-mm) semicircles (see tip on page 242)
- 12 ounces (340 g) carrots, cut diagonally into 2-inch (5-cm) pieces
- 1 (15.5-oz/439-g) can chickpeas, rinsed
- 2 romaine hearts, thinly sliced
- 4 ounces (115 g) blue cheese, crumbled
- ¼ cup Quick-Pickled Red Onions (page 222)
- 2 tablespoons red wine vinegar

HOW TO MAKE IT

Preheat your oven to 450°F (230°C).

Mix 2 tablespoons of the oil, the cumin, coriander, 2 teaspoons salt, and 1 teaspoon pepper in a large bowl. Add the squash, carrots, and chickpeas and use a spatula to make sure the vegetables and chickpeas are evenly coated with the oil and spices. Divide evenly between two rimmed baking sheets and smooth into one layer.

Roast the vegetables for 12 to 15 minutes, tossing once, until golden brown and you can easily pierce a piece of squash with a fork. The chickpeas should be crispy. Let the vegetables and chickpeas cool slightly so they won't wilt the lettuce.

Divide the romaine and vegetables between the serving bowls. Top with the cheese and onions, then drizzle with the remaining 2 tablespoons oil and the vinegar. Sprinkle the bowls with ½ teaspoon each salt and pepper and eat right away!

Brown Rice and Adzuki Bean Bowls

MAKES DINNER FOR 4

Want to know one little trick to make your life easier? Use a big enough bowl when you're mixing the slaw. That way little bits don't fly out onto the counter and you have space to toss the ingredients evenly.

INGREDIENTS

- ½ large Napa cabbage head (12 oz/340 g), sliced (6½ cups)
- 3 small carrots, shaved with a vegetable peeler
- 1 cup (100 g) sugar snap peas, sliced
- 2 tablespoons sesame seeds, plus more for serving
- ½ cup Toasted Sesame and Miso Dressing (page 229)
- 1 cup (6¾ oz/190 g) short-grain brown rice, rinsed
- Kosher salt
- 2 tablespoons chopped fresh cilantro leaves, plus more for serving
- 1 (15-oz/425-g) can adzuki or small red beans, rinsed
- 2 avocados, sliced
- 1 small fresh red chile, sliced

HOW TO MAKE IT

Bring a large pot of water to a boil. While it comes to a boil, mix the cabbage, carrots, snap peas, and sesame seeds in a large bowl with ¼ cup (60 ml) of the dressing. Use your hands to make sure everything gets evenly coated, or use a spatula. Set aside and toss occasionally.

Once the water is boiling, add the rice and 1 tablespoon kosher salt. Reduce to a simmer and cook until the rice is just tender, 22 to 26 minutes. Drain.

Just before serving, fold the cilantro into the cabbage salad. Divide the rice, cabbage salad, beans, and avocados among four bowls. Drizzle with the remaining ¼ cup dressing, and sprinkle with the chile and more cilantro and sesame seeds, if you like.

CHAPTER 6

Chicken + Turkey

I wonder how many recipes there are in the world for chicken dinners. One billion, perhaps? So, when I was creating *Healthyish* chicken recipes, it was important to me that I offer something helpful, new, and delicious, whether that's transforming store-bought rotisserie chicken into quick tacos or teaching you how to roast juicy (never dry) boneless chicken breasts.

And, in general, I believe we could do well with a little less meat. It's good for the planet, and it's also good for your wallet. Serving sizes hover between 4 to 6 ounces per person in the Turkey and Chickpea Burgers (page 155) and in the Chicken and Greens Sauté with Peanut Sauce (page 151). Making up for the difference with chickpeas and vegetables stretches the meat further, and is less caloric. Win-win.

←
**Coriander-Rubbed
Chicken Breasts with
Lentil-Radicchio Salad**
PAGE 146

Quick Rotisserie Chicken Tacos with Smashed Avocado

MAKES DINNER FOR 4

Use any remaining rotisserie chicken in Tangy Chicken Salad Tartine (page 87) or add to Roasted Vegetable and Barley Bowls (page 135).

INGREDIENTS

- 1 avocado, chopped
- 1 tablespoon fresh lime juice, plus wedges for serving
- ¼ teaspoon crushed red pepper flakes, plus more for serving

  Kosher salt and freshly ground black pepper
- 8 corn tortillas
- ½ of 2- to 2½-pound (907-g to 1.2-kg) rotisserie chicken, shredded
- 1 cup (240 ml) store-bought salsa verde or pico de gallo
- 3 ounces (85 g) Cotija cheese, crumbled, or extra-sharp Cheddar cheese, shredded
- ¼ cup Quick-Pickled Red Onions (page 222)

  Fresh cilantro leaves, for serving

HOW TO MAKE IT

Mash the avocado with the lime juice, red pepper flakes, and ¼ teaspoon each salt and black pepper in a small bowl.

Using tongs, toast each tortilla directly on the grate of a gas burner turned to medium-high. Cook, flipping once, until the edges are charred and the tortilla is hot. If you don't have a gas burner, microwave the tortillas until hot, 15 to 30 seconds.

Spread the mashed avocado on the toasted tortillas, dividing it equally. Top with the chicken, salsa, cheese, and pickled onions. Sprinkle with cilantro leaves, red pepper flakes, and additional salt. Serve with lime wedges alongside.

Coriander-Rubbed Chicken Breasts with Lentil-Radicchio Salad

MAKES DINNER FOR 4

The key to juicy boneless, skinless chicken breasts? Adding a bit of water to the pan and covering while they bake. This creates steam so they remain moist, not dry. Cooking time for breasts varies on thickness, so I give a wide range. If you want to cool the lentils quickly, spread them out on a rimmed baking sheet.

INGREDIENTS

- 4 boneless, skinless chicken breasts (2½ to 3 lbs/1.2 to 1.4 kg total)
- 2 tablespoons olive oil
- 2 teaspoons ground coriander

  Kosher salt and freshly ground black pepper
- 1 cup (200 g) French green lentils (Puy lentils), rinsed
- ¼ cup (60 ml) water
- 1 medium head radicchio, halved crosswise and sliced ½ inch (12 mm) thick
- 2 Persian cucumbers, thinly sliced
- 2 ounces (55 g) feta cheese, crumbled
- ¼ cup chopped fresh parsley leaves, plus more for serving
- 2 tablespoons store-bought preserved lemon, chopped
- ⅓ cup Creamy Tahini Dressing (page 232)

HOW TO MAKE IT

Preheat your oven to 375°F (190°C).

In a 9 by 13-inch (20 by 30-cm) baking dish, toss the chicken breasts with the oil, coriander, 2 teaspoons salt, and 1 teaspoon pepper. Set aside to marinate while the oven heats.

Meanwhile, bring a medium pot of water to a boil. Add the lentils and salt the water. Reduce to a simmer, cover, and cook until the lentils are just tender, 16 to 20 minutes. Drain, rinse, and let cool to room temperature.

When the oven is hot, add the water to the baking dish, cover with foil, and bake the chicken until an instant-read thermometer inserted into the thickest part of the breast registers 160°F (72°C), 22 to 28 minutes. Let the chicken rest for 5 minutes to absorb any juices, and to allow it reach 165°F (74°C).

Toss the cooled lentils with the radicchio, cucumbers, feta, parsley, preserved lemon, and ¼ cup of the dressing. Season to taste with additional salt and pepper.

Slice the chicken and serve over the salad, sprinkled with extra parsley leaves and drizzled with the remaining dressing.

Spiced Chicken and Chickpea Flatbreads with Cucumber-Dill Tzatziki

MAKES DINNER FOR 4

If you have leftovers, this dinner makes a delicious lunch for the next day. Shred the chicken and tear up the toasted flatbread into bite-size pieces. Toss them with some of the arugula and dressing to make a "fattoush," also known as a pita bread salad.

INGREDIENTS

- 1 pound (455 g) boneless, skinless chicken thighs
- 1 (15.5-oz/439-g) can chickpeas, rinsed
- 1 tablespoon plus 2 teaspoons canola or vegetable oil
- 1 teaspoon ground cumin
- 1 teaspoon ground coriander
- Kosher salt and freshly ground black pepper
- 4 pieces whole-grain flatbread or pitas
- ¾ cup Cucumber-Dill Tzatziki (page 234)
- 6 cups (5 oz/120 g) arugula leaves
- Chopped fresh dill, for serving

HOW TO MAKE IT

Preheat your oven to 425°F (220°F).

Put the chicken and chickpeas on a rimmed baking sheet. Drizzle with 1 tablespoon of the oil and sprinkle with the cumin, coriander, and 1 teaspoon each salt and pepper. Use your hands to rub the spices into both sides of the chicken and the chickpeas. (If you are squeamish about touching raw chicken with your hands, use tongs to flip the chicken and season evenly.)

Make sure everything is in a single layer on the baking sheet and roast in the preheated oven, tossing once, until the chicken is cooked through and the chickpeas are crispy, 14 to 16 minutes. Let rest for 5 minutes, then transfer the chicken to a medium bowl and use two forks to tear the chicken into bite-size chunks.

Drizzle the remaining 2 teaspoons oil over the chickpeas and then smash with a potato masher or fork.

Just before serving, toast the flatbreads. Top each with the tzatziki, arugula, chicken, chickpeas, and fresh dill and season with salt and pepper.

Chicken and Greens Sauté with Peanut Sauce

MAKES DINNER FOR 4 TO 6

I love stir-fries, but they are often too greasy for my taste. Using boneless, skinless chicken thighs adds richness without relying on a lot of oil or adding rendered fat from the chicken skin. I prefer baby bok choy to larger bunches because they have a fresher taste, but any equivalent weight will work.

INGREDIENTS

- 6 boneless, skinless chicken thighs (1½ lbs/680 g), cut into 1-inch (2.5-cm) cubes
- 2 tablespoons soy sauce
- 2 tablespoons canola or vegetable oil
- 1 bunch scallions, thinly sliced, light and dark green parts separated
- 2 pounds (910 g) baby bok choy, stems removed and sliced into 1-inch (2.5-cm) pieces
- ¼ cup (60 ml) water
- 3 tablespoons rice vinegar
- 3 cups of your favorite cooked whole grains (page 236), heated
- ½ cup Sweet-Hot Peanut Sauce (page 233)
- ¼ cup (35 g) chopped roasted peanuts
- 1 small fresh red chile, thinly sliced

HOW TO MAKE IT

Toss the chicken with 1 tablespoon of the soy sauce. Heat the oil in a large nonstick skillet over medium-high heat. Add the chicken and cook, turning the chicken pieces occasionally, until golden brown and almost cooked through, 8 to 10 minutes. Transfer the chicken to a plate and cover loosely with foil to keep warm while you cook the greens.

Add the scallions and cook until softened, 2 to 3 minutes. Stir in the bok choy and water, cover, and cook, stirring occasionally, until wilted and tender, 6 to 10 minutes (this will depend on how hearty the bok choy is).

Stir in the vinegar and the remaining 1 tablespoon soy sauce. Return the chicken to the skillet to coat. Serve over the grains, drizzled with the peanut sauce and sprinkled with the peanuts and sliced chile.

Roasted Curried Chicken and Grape Salad

MAKES DINNER FOR 4

This has all the flavors of curry chicken salad without an overly rich mayonnaise dressing.

INGREDIENTS

- 6 boneless, skinless chicken thighs (about 1½ lbs/680 g total)
- 12 ounces (340 g) small broccoli florets from 1 medium head broccoli (1¼ to 1½ lbs/570 to 680 g)
- 2 cups (12 oz/340 g) red grapes, halved
- 2 teaspoons curry powder
- 3 tablespoons canola oil

  Kosher salt and freshly ground black pepper
- 3 tablespoons fresh lime juice
- 2 large heads Bibb or Boston lettuce, torn into bite-size pieces
- ½ cup fresh cilantro leaves, torn
- ⅓ cup (45 g) roasted, unsalted cashews, chopped
- ¼ cup unsweetened coconut flakes, toasted (see tip on page 242)

HOW TO MAKE IT

Preheat your oven to 400°F (205°C) with the two racks positioned in the top and bottom slots.

Toss the chicken, broccoli, grapes, curry powder, 1 tablespoon of the oil, and 1 teaspoon each salt and pepper in a large bowl. Divide the mixture between two rimmed baking sheets. Roast, tossing once, until the chicken is golden and cooked through, 18 to 20 minutes. Remove the baking sheets from the oven and let cool slightly. When cool enough to handle, shred the chicken into bite-size pieces using 2 forks.

Just before serving, whisk the remaining 2 tablespoons oil, the lime juice, and ¼ teaspoon each salt and pepper in a large serving bowl. Fold in the lettuce and divide among serving bowls. Top each bowl with the chicken, grapes, and broccoli, dividing them equally, then sprinkle with the cilantro, cashews, and coconut flakes. Season with salt and pepper and serve.

Turkey and Chickpea Burgers with Dill Havarti

MAKES DINNER FOR 4 TO 6

These burgers are the epitome of *Healthyish* cooking. You still get a juicy turkey burger taste, but a can of chickpeas stretches the meat further. Freeze extra patties on a parchment paper–lined baking sheet or plate, and then transfer to an airtight container for up to 2 months. Defrost completely before cooking.

INGREDIENTS

1 (15.5-oz/439-g) can chickpeas, rinsed

1 pound (455 g) 90-percent lean ground turkey

½ cup (40 g) panko bread crumbs

1 large egg, beaten

1 tablespoon Dijon mustard

1 tablespoon Worcestershire sauce

1 garlic clove, chopped

3 tablespoons olive oil

Kosher salt and freshly ground black pepper

6 ounces (170 g) sliced dill havarti cheese or Muenster cheese

Toasted buns, mayonnaise, mustard, lettuce, and sliced tomato, for serving

HOW TO MAKE IT

Line a baking sheet with parchment paper; set aside.

Mash the chickpeas in a large bowl until there are no whole chickpeas left. Using your hands, mix in the turkey, bread crumbs, egg, mustard, Worcestershire sauce, garlic, 1 tablespoon of the oil, 2 teaspoons salt, and 1 teaspoon pepper. Form four to six 1-inch-thick (2.5-cm) patties (about ½ cup each) and place on the lined baking sheet.

Heat the remaining 2 tablespoons oil in a large nonstick skillet over medium heat. Add the patties and cook until golden brown and opaque throughout, 3 to 4 minutes per side. Top each patty with a slice of cheese, cover, and cook until the cheese has melted, about 1 minute. (You can also do this in batches.)

Serve the burgers on toasted buns with mayonnaise, mustard, lettuce, and tomato slices.

Paprika-Rubbed Chicken Thighs with Smashed Cauliflower

MAKES DINNER FOR 4

The key to getting crispy chicken thighs is to give them enough room in the pan, and—this is important—to not touch them until they're done. Take my word for it and set a timer for 6 minutes, and that is when you check by lifting the skin. If there are leftovers, I like to shred the chicken and toss it with the cauliflower, baby arugula, and some capers.

INGREDIENTS

2 teaspoons smoked paprika

2 teaspoons dried oregano

2 teaspoons crushed fennel seeds

Kosher salt and freshly ground black pepper

8 small bone-in, skin-on chicken thighs (2½ to 3 lbs/1.2 to 1.4 kg total)

1 tablespoon olive oil

1 large cauliflower (about 3 lbs/1.4 kg), cut into small florets

2 tablespoons chopped fresh flat-leaf parsley leaves, plus more for serving

1 tablespoon white wine vinegar

HOW TO MAKE IT

Preheat your oven to 425°F (220°C) with a rack positioned in the middle of the oven.

Mix the paprika, oregano, fennel seeds, 2 teaspoons salt, and 1 teaspoon pepper in a small bowl. Dab any moisture from the chicken with a paper towel. Sprinkle the spices over the chicken, and toss with tongs or your hands until evenly coated with spices.

Heat the oil in your largest ovenproof skillet over medium-high heat. Add half the thighs, skin-side down, and cook (without touching!) until the skin is crispy, 8 to 10 minutes. Transfer the first batch to a plate and repeat with the remaining chicken. Reduce the heat if the skin is starting to burn.

Drain all but 1 tablespoon of the fat from the skillet, add the cauliflower, and toss to coat in the oil. Place the chicken on top of the cauliflower, skin-side up. Transfer the skillet to the oven and cook for 18 to 24 minutes, until an instant-read thermometer inserted in the center of one of the chicken thighs registers 165°F (74°C).

Transfer the chicken to a serving plate, and, using a potato masher, smash the cauliflower into bite-size pieces. Stir in the parsley, vinegar, and ½ teaspoon each salt and pepper. Serve the chicken over the cauliflower, sprinkled with extra parsley.

One-Pot Spicy and Creamy Chicken Pasta

MAKES DINNER FOR 4

When you're using whole-wheat or whole-grain pasta, high quality makes all the difference. (My favorite brands are Sfoglini and Rustichella d'Abruzzo.) And, I know, I'm asking you to chop a lot of herbs here. I like a hefty portion because it cuts the richness of the sauce. However, if you go with just parsley and basil, it's quick to get to ½ cup.

INGREDIENTS

- 2 tablespoons unsalted butter
- 2 large shallots, very thinly sliced
- 1 teaspoon Aleppo pepper or crushed red pepper flakes, plus more for serving

  Kosher salt and freshly ground black pepper
- 12 ounces (340 g) short whole-wheat pasta (I like rigatoni or macaroni best)
- 2 cups (390 g) shredded chicken and 4 cups (960 ml) chicken stock from Whole Poached Chicken (page 241), or water
- ¼ cup (60 ml) heavy cream
- ½ cup chopped mixed fresh herbs, such as oregano, parsley, sage, and basil, plus more for serving
- 2 tablespoons fresh lemon juice, plus 1 teaspoon lemon zest

HOW TO MAKE IT

Heat the butter in a large skillet over medium heat. Add the shallots, Aleppo pepper, 2 teaspoons salt, and 1 teaspoon pepper. Cook, stirring frequently, until the shallots are soft and golden, 5 to 8 minutes.

Stir in the pasta and stock or water, cover, and bring to a boil. Remove the lid and cook, stirring frequently and making sure there's no pasta stuck to the bottom of the pot, until the pasta is almost tender and cooked through, 8 to 12 minutes. (This will depend on the brand you're using.) Stir in the chicken and cream and cook until heated through, 1 to 2 minutes more. Stir in the herbs, lemon juice, and lemon zest and season with ¼ teaspoon salt.

Serve hot, sprinkled with more herbs and Aleppo pepper.

157

One-Pan Crispy Chicken with Herbed Potatoes and Onions

MAKES DINNER FOR 4

I love this kind of recipe—you put in 15 minutes of prep work on the front end, and then sit back and relax while the oven does the rest. If you want to pick just one herb, I suggest rosemary.

INGREDIENTS

- 2½ to 3 pounds (1.2 to 1.4 kg) new potatoes, cut into ½-inch (12-mm) pieces (about 8 cups)
- 1 medium onion, diced
- 2 (6-in/15-cm) fresh rosemary branches
- 10 fresh thyme sprigs
- 5 fresh oregano sprigs
- 1 lemon, thinly sliced
- Kosher salt and freshly ground black pepper
- 2 tablespoons Dijon mustard
- 2 tablespoons unsalted butter, at room temperature
- 4 chicken legs (about 3 lbs/1.4 kg total)

HOW TO MAKE IT

Preheat your oven to 425°F (220°C), with a rack positioned in the top of the oven.

Toss the potatoes, onion, rosemary, thyme, oregano, lemon, and 1 teaspoon each salt and pepper in a 9 by 13-inch (20 by 30-cm) baking dish. Set aside.

Mix the mustard and butter together in a small bowl. Gently loosen the skin of the chicken and rub the mustard-butter underneath. Season the chicken legs with 1 teaspoon salt and ½ teaspoon pepper. Place the chicken legs on top of the potatoes and nestle them in so they're secure. Roast until an instant-read thermometer inserted in the thickest part of the chicken registers 160°F (72°C) and the potatoes are golden brown and tender, 50 minutes to 1 hour.

Remove from the oven and let rest for 5 minutes before serving. This allows the chicken to reach 165°F (74°C) and for the juices to redistribute. Serve hot.

CHAPTER 7

Pork and Beef

I think of this chapter as my steak-and-potatoes offering to *Healthyish* cooks. They're crowd pleasers for most meat eaters—straightforward flavors in a variety of dishes. That being said, each recipe includes a way to try something new: I suggest Juicy Pork Chops with Sweet Potato, Fennel, and Apple Hash (page 164) for impressing the in-laws or Bahn Mi Rice Bowls with Spicy Pork and Sriracha Mayo (page 170) if you're interested in trying your hand at a new ingredient like fish sauce.

←
**Bahn Mi Rice Bowls
with Spicy Pork and
Sriracha Mayo**
PAGE 170

Pork Tenderloin and Carrots with Tangy Romaine Salad

MAKES DINNER FOR 4

Pork tenderloins vary in thickness, so start checking the temperature at 20 minutes.

INGREDIENTS

- 1 pound (455 g) carrots, cut into 3-inch (7.5-cm) pieces
- 3 tablespoons olive oil
- Kosher salt and freshly ground black pepper
- 1¼ to 1½ pounds (570 to 680 g) pork tenderloin
- 1 teaspoon chili powder
- ½ teaspoon ground cumin
- 2 tablespoons fresh lime juice
- 2 romaine hearts, shredded
- ½ cup fresh cilantro leaves, plus more for serving
- ½ cup (65 g) roasted pumpkin seeds, plus more for serving
- 1 avocado, chopped

HOW TO MAKE IT

Preheat your oven to 425°F (220°C), with a rack positioned in the highest slot.

On a rimmed baking sheet, toss the carrots with 1 tablespoon of the oil, ½ teaspoon kosher salt, and ¼ teaspoon pepper. Season the pork with the chili powder, cumin, 1 teaspoon salt, and ½ teaspoon pepper and nestle in the carrots.

Roast, tossing the carrots and turning the pork once, until an instant-read thermometer inserted into the center of the pork registers 140°F (60°C), 20 to 26 minutes. Let rest for 10 minutes to allow the juices to redistribute and reach 145°F (63°C) while you make the salad, then slice.

Just before serving, assemble the salad. Whisk the remaining 2 tablespoons oil with the lime juice, ½ teaspoon salt, and ¼ teaspoon pepper. Add the romaine, cilantro, and pumpkin seeds and toss to combine. Gently fold in the avocado.

Serve the pork and carrots with the salad, sprinkled with more cilantro, pumpkin seeds, and salt.

Juicy Pork Chops with Sweet Potato, Fennel, and Apple Hash

MAKES DINNER FOR 4

My method for pan-roasting pork chops ensures you won't end up with a dry hockey puck.

INGREDIENTS

¼ cup (60 ml) olive oil

1 pound (455 g) large fennel bulb, cut into ½-inch (12-mm) pieces (about 2 cups)

1 pound (455 g) sweet potatoes, cut into ½-inch (12-mm) pieces (about 3 cups)

2 tart apples, such as Pink Lady or Fuji, cut into ½-inch (12-mm) pieces

Kosher salt and freshly ground black pepper

3 tablespoons fresh orange juice, plus 1 teaspoon zest

1 teaspoon chopped fresh sage leaves, plus leaves for serving

4 bone-in, 1-inch-thick (2.5-cm) pork chops (about 2½ lbs/1.2 kg total)

2 teaspoons crushed fennel seeds

½ teaspoon crushed red pepper flakes, plus more for serving

HOW TO MAKE IT

Heat 2 tablespoons of the oil in a large skillet over medium-high heat. Add the fennel, sweet potatoes, apples, 1 teaspoon salt, and ½ teaspoon pepper. Cook, stirring often, until the sweet potatoes are fork-tender, 14 to 18 minutes. Stir in the orange juice, orange zest, and chopped sage.

Meanwhile, heat the remaining 2 tablespoons oil in a large skillet over medium-high heat. Season the pork with the fennel seeds, red pepper flakes, and 2 teaspoons each salt and black pepper.

Cook, turning once, until an instant-read thermometer inserted into the thickest part registers 140°F (60°C), 3 to 4 minutes per side. Let rest 5 minutes to allow the juices to redistribute and reach 145°F (63°C). Serve the pork chops with the hash alongside, drizzled with any pan juices and sprinkled with red pepper flakes, sage leaves, and salt.

Cuminy Pork Cutlets with Smashed Butternut Squash

MAKES DINNER FOR 4 TO 6

This rich-tasting dinner is both dairy- and gluten-free. To pound the pork thin, wrap a cutlet loosely with plastic wrap and place on your cutting board. Using a meat mallet, pound the pork cutlets until they're ¼ inch (6 mm) thick. Repeat with the remaining cutlets. If you don't have a meat mallet, use a rolling pin.

INGREDIENTS

1 large butternut squash (about 3½ lbs/1.6 kg), peeled and cut into 2-inch (5-cm) chunks

1½ teaspoons ground cumin

1 teaspoon smoked paprika

Kosher salt and freshly ground black pepper

4 pork cutlets (about 1 lb/455 g total), pounded to ¼-inch (6-mm) thickness

¼ cup (60 ml) olive oil

2 tablespoons fresh lime juice

¼ cup chopped fresh cilantro leaves

2 tablespoons Quick-Pickled Red Onions (page 222)

HOW TO MAKE IT

Fill a steamer pot with 1 inch (2.5 cm) of water and fit with the steamer insert. Cover and bring to a boil, then add the butternut squash. Cook until you can easily poke a piece of butternut squash with a fork, 15 to 18 minutes.

Meanwhile, in a small bowl, mix together the cumin, smoked paprika, and 1 teaspoon each salt and pepper. Sprinkle the mixture evenly over the pork cutlets, making sure both sides are evenly coated.

Heat 2 tablespoons of the oil in a large skillet over medium-high heat. Add the pork and cook until cooked through, 1 to 2 minutes per side. Do this in batches, if necessary. Transfer the pork to a plate and let rest for 5 minutes, covered with aluminum foil to keep warm.

When the squash is done cooking, transfer it to a serving bowl and mash with a potato masher. Stir in 1 tablespoon of the oil, ½ teaspoon salt, and ¼ teaspoon pepper.

Stir together the remaining 1 tablespoon oil, the lime juice, cilantro, pickled onions, and ¼ teaspoon each salt and pepper. Serve the cutlets over the squash, topped with the cilantro-lime sauce.

Sausage, Potato, and Cabbage One-Pot Dinner

MAKES DINNER FOR 4

I'm going to be real with you—this isn't a particularly quick dinner. But it does happen in just one pot, and it's relatively hands-off once you get the cooking started. If you can't find Yukon Gold potatoes, use fingerling potatoes since they're also waxy (not starchy) potatoes. Bratwurst is ideal here for its mild flavor, but any lightly seasoned pork sausage will work, too.

INGREDIENTS

3   slices thick-cut bacon (about 4 oz/115 g)

1   large yellow onion, very thinly sliced

1   teaspoon caraway seeds

    Kosher salt and freshly ground black pepper

1   cup (240 ml) dry white wine, such as dry Riesling, pinot grigio, or sauvignon blanc

1   medium head cabbage (2½ lbs/ 1.2 kg), quartered and cut into ½-inch (12-mm) slices

1   cup (240 ml) chicken stock from Whole Poached Chicken (page 241), or Vegetable Stock (page 239)

4   large bratwurst sausage links (1 lb/455 g total)

6   medium Yukon Gold potatoes (2 lbs/910 g), chopped into 1-inch (2.5-cm) pieces

¼   to ⅓ cup (60 to 80 g) Dijon mustard

¼   to ⅓ cup chopped fresh flat-leaf parsley leaves from 1 small bunch

HOW TO MAKE IT

Heat a large pot over medium-low heat. Place the bacon slices flat in the pot and cook, turning a couple times, until crispy and most of the fat has drained from the bacon, 8 to 12 minutes. Transfer the bacon to a plate, leaving the fat in the pot. Let the bacon cool, then cut into ¾-inch (2-cm) pieces.

Add the onions, caraway seeds, and 1 teaspoon each salt and pepper to the pot. Cook, stirring often, until the onions are completely soft, 10 to 12 minutes. Pour in the white wine and use a flat-bottomed spatula to scrape the meaty bits off the bottom of the pot. Continue to scrape until the wine has reduced by about half, 3 to 5 minutes.

Stir in the cabbage and stock, cover, and cook, stirring occasionally, until the cabbage is very soft, 20 to 25 minutes. Stir in the chopped bacon and then nestle the sausages in the cabbage so they are completely covered. Add the potatoes on top, in an even layer. Sprinkle with 1 teaspoon salt and re-cover. Cook over medium-low heat until the potatoes are fork-tender and the sausage is cooked through, 18 to 22 minutes more.

Spoon the potatoes, cabbage, sausage, and any juices into serving bowls. Season with salt and pepper, dollop with mustard, sprinkle with the parsley, and eat hot.

Bahn Mi Rice Bowls with Spicy Pork and Sriracha Mayo

MAKES DINNER FOR 4

I love a bahn mi sandwich—the pillowy bread, rich ham, pork pâté, and sour pickled vegetables that cut through the richness. This plays off those same flavors, but with a base of brown rice instead of baguette.

INGREDIENTS

- 1 large carrot, shredded (about ½ cup/55 g)
- 3 Persian cucumbers, halved and cut into thin matchsticks
- 3 tablespoons rice vinegar
- 2 tablespoons fish sauce
- 1 tablespoon plus 1 teaspoon canola oil
- 1 teaspoon granulated sugar
- 1 pound (455 g) lean ground pork
  Kosher salt
- 1 bunch scallions, thinly sliced
- 3 garlic cloves, finely chopped
- ⅓ cup (75 ml) mayonnaise
- 1 tablespoon sriracha, or another hot chili sauce
- 3 cups (585 g) cooked brown rice (page 237)
- ¼ cup fresh cilantro leaves

HOW TO MAKE IT

Toss the carrots, cucumbers, 2 tablespoons of the vinegar, 1 tablespoon of the fish sauce, 1 teaspoon of the oil, and ½ teaspoon of the sugar in a medium bowl. Set aside, tossing occasionally, while you cook the pork. The vegetables should soften and wilt slightly.

Heat the remaining 1 tablespoon oil in a large skillet over medium-high heat. Add the pork and ½ teaspoon salt. Cook, breaking it up with a spoon into small pieces, until golden brown and cooked through, 6 to 8 minutes. Stir in the scallions and cook until softened, 2 to 3 minutes. Add the garlic and cook until fragrant, about 1 minute more. Stir in the remaining 1 tablespoon fish sauce, 1 tablespoon vinegar, and ½ teaspoon sugar.

Stir together the mayonnaise and sriracha. Serve the rice topped with the pork and any juices from the pan, the carrot-cucumber pickles, sriracha mayo, and cilantro.

Skirt Steak with Corn, Potato, and Smoked Mozzarella Salad

MAKES DINNER FOR 4

Credit goes to my mom for this clever combination of mozzarella, corn, and steamed potatoes. It's beige on beige, but don't let that sway you. Raw corn adds a pop of sweet among the smoky cheese and tart dressing. You can steam the potatoes up to two days in advance and assemble the entire potato salad up to 8 hours ahead of time. If you do this, add the herbs just before serving.

INGREDIENTS

- 1½ pounds (680 g) fingerling potatoes, halved or cut into quarters if large
- 1 tablespoon olive oil
- 1½ pounds (680 g) skirt steak
- 1 teaspoon dried oregano
- Kosher salt and freshly ground black pepper
- 2 cups (290 g) corn kernels, from 2 cobs (see tip on page 242)
- 4 ounces (115 g) smoked mozzarella, cut into ½-inch (12-mm) cubes
- ⅓ cup Cidery Dijon Vinaigrette (page 233)
- 2 tablespoons chopped fresh flat-leaf parsley leaves
- 2 tablespoons chopped fresh basil leaves
- 2 tablespoons chopped fresh chives

HOW TO MAKE IT

Fill a steamer pot with 1 inch (2.5 cm) of water and fit with the steamer insert. Cover, bring to a boil, and add the potatoes. Cook until the potatoes can be easily poked with a fork, 14 to 18 minutes. Set aside to cool to room temperature while you cook the steak.

Heat the oil in a large skillet over medium-high heat. Put the steak on a plate and sprinkle it evenly with the oregano and 1 teaspoon each salt and pepper. For medium-rare, cook the steak until an instant-read thermometer inserted into the thickest part of the steak registers 130°F (55°C), 2 to 4 minutes per side. (Go a little longer on each side if you like your steak cooked more.)

Transfer the steak to a cutting board and tent with aluminum foil. Let the steak rest for 5 minutes to allow the juices to redistribute and reach a temperature of 135°F (57°C) before slicing.

Toss the cooled potatoes with the corn, mozzarella, vinaigrette, parsley, basil, chives, 1½ teaspoons salt, and 1 teaspoon pepper. Serve with the steak.

Hanger Steak with Roasted Acorn Squash

MAKES DINNER FOR 4 TO 6

One of the essential tenets of a *Healthyish* meal is beauty. Food that looks good probably tastes good, too. After all, we eat with our eyes first. This meal lives up to that promise with jewel-toned orange and purples and a pop of green sauce on top of juicy steak.

INGREDIENTS

- 2 large acorn squashes (3 lbs/1.4 kg total), halved, seeded, and cut into 1½-inch (4-cm) wedges
- 2 medium red onions, peeled and quartered through the stem and petals pulled apart
- 5 tablespoons (75 ml) olive oil

  Kosher salt and freshly ground black pepper
- 1¾ pounds (800 g) hanger steak, halved through the center membrane if still attached, and cut into pieces that will fit your pan
- ¼ teaspoon cayenne pepper
- 2 garlic cloves, 1 crushed and 1 minced
- ¼ cup chopped fresh chives
- 3 tablespoons fresh lemon juice, plus 1 teaspoon finely grated zest

HOW TO MAKE IT

Preheat your oven to 425°F (220°C), with racks positioned in the top and bottom thirds of the oven.

Divide the squash and onions between two rimmed baking sheets. Drizzle with 2 tablespoons of the oil and 1 teaspoon each salt and pepper. Roast, tossing once and rotating the pans top to bottom and front to back, until you can easily insert a fork into the squash, 25 to 30 minutes.

Meanwhile, put the steak in a bowl and season with the cayenne, the crushed garlic clove and 1 teaspoon each salt and pepper. Ten minutes before the vegetables come out of the oven, heat 1 tablespoon of the remaining oil in a large skillet over medium-high heat. Add the steak to the pan, making sure there's space in between the pieces so they don't steam. Cook the steak until desired doneness, 6 to 8 minutes for medium-rare. Let the steak rest while you make the sauce.

Stir together the chives, lemon juice and lemon zest, the minced garlic clove, the remaining 2 tablespoons oil, ½ teaspoon salt, and ¼ teaspoon pepper.

Serve the steak drizzled with the sauce, with the vegetables alongside. Season with salt and additional pepper, if you like.

Pork and Mushroom Stroganoff

MAKES DINNER FOR 4

This flips the script on traditional beef stroganoff and makes mushrooms the center star with pork (instead of beef) in a supporting role.

INGREDIENTS

Kosher salt and freshly ground black pepper

1 tablespoon olive oil

½ pound (225 g) ground pork

1 pound (455 g) button mushrooms, sliced (about 6 cups)

3 medium shallots, thinly sliced (about 1½ cups/175 g)

3 garlic cloves, chopped

12 ounces (340 g) whole-wheat fettuccine or linguine

¼ packed cup chopped fresh flat-leaf parsley leaves

¼ cup (60 ml) sour cream

2 tablespoons fresh lemon juice

HOW TO MAKE IT

Bring a large pot of water to a boil and salt it generously—1 tablespoon should do.

While the water comes to a boil, heat the oil in a large skillet over medium-high heat. Add the pork and season with ¾ teaspoon each salt and pepper. Cook, stirring occasionally and breaking up clumps, until the pork is golden brown and cooked through, 6 to 8 minutes. Use a slotted spoon to transfer the pork to a shallow bowl. Leave the fat in the pan.

Add the mushrooms to the pan along with the shallots, garlic, 1 teaspoon salt, and ¼ teaspoon pepper. Cook over high heat, stirring often, until the mushrooms are golden brown and the shallots are tender, 10 to 12 minutes. Continue to cook over high heat to let any liquid evaporate and the mushrooms to brown.

While the mushrooms cook, add the pasta to the water and cook until just barely tender; the timing will depend on the brand of pasta you bought. Using a heatproof liquid measuring cup, scoop out 1 cup (240 ml) of the pasta cooking water and reserve. Drain the pasta.

Add the pasta, pork, and the reserved pasta water to the pan. Toss constantly with tongs over medium heat until the pasta is completely cooked through, 2 to 3 minutes more. Remove from the heat and stir in the parsley, sour cream, and lemon juice. Season with ½ teaspoon salt and ¼ teaspoon pepper. Serve hot.

When in doubt, choose whole grains: Swap in brown rice for white, or multigrain toast for sourdough.

CHAPTER 8

Fish and Shrimp

Of all the categories of proteins, I think fish intimidates home cooks the most. Not only is fish expensive, fear of over- or undercooking has scared many people away.

So, half of this chapter helps you try your hand at cooking salmon, swordfish, and Arctic char in low-stakes environments. Using my methods, you can sear salmon and get a deliciously crispy skin. I promise! Poaching bass ensures tender, flavorful fish, and broiling thin fillets of char is not only fast, but foolproof.

The remaining recipes make use of pantry staples— if you've got a can of tuna or a tin of sardines, you're not too far away from dinner.

With any animal protein, but with fish in particular, look for sustainably raised sources. Labels like MSC-certified will help you determine whether the fish was caught or harvested responsibly.

←
Broiled Arctic Char with Marinated Cucumber and Radish Salad
PAGE 188

Simple Salmon and Quinoa Bowl

MAKES DINNER FOR 4

This is a fish dish that feels particularly light and, well, not *too* fishy thanks to the tangy yogurt, nutty quinoa, and fresh dill. Do not disturb the fillets while they cook on the skin side—you want to make sure they get a lovely golden brown crust.

INGREDIENTS

Kosher salt and freshly ground black pepper

1 cup (170 g) quinoa, rinsed

4 (6-oz/170-g) skin-on salmon fillets

1½ teaspoons ground coriander

1 tablespoon olive oil

1 medium head Bibb lettuce, torn into bite-size pieces (about 6 cups/330 g)

1 cup Cucumber-Dill Tzatziki (page 234)

Chopped fresh dill and lemon wedges, for serving

HOW TO MAKE IT

Bring a small pot of water to a rolling boil. Salt the water and add the quinoa. Reduce to a strong simmer and cook until the quinoa is chewy but not soft, 11 to 13 minutes. Drain.

Meanwhile, cook the salmon. In a small bowl, mix together the coriander, 2 teaspoons salt, and 1 teaspoon pepper. Season the salmon on both sides with the spice mixture.

Heat the oil in a large nonstick skillet over medium heat. Add the salmon, skin side down, and cook without disturbing until the skin is golden brown and crispy, 5 to 7 minutes. Flip the fillets and cook until opaque throughout, 1 to 3 minutes more, depending on your desired doneness.

Serve the salmon and quinoa over the lettuce, dolloped with the tzatziki and sprinkled with the dill. Serve with lemon wedges.

Baked Swordfish with Tomatoes, Corn, and Green Beans

MAKES DINNER FOR 4

I love this hands-off method for cooking fish. Since you're cooking the swordfish slow and low in a steam environment, there's no worry that it'll go from juicy to dry in just a few seconds. The fish will still look a little underdone in the middle when you pull it out—it should be opaque but slightly pink. I buy sustainable, MSC-certified frozen swordfish from my grocery store and defrost when I'm planning to cook them.

INGREDIENTS

- 3 small tomatoes (8 oz/225 g), cut into quarters
- 12 ounces (340 g) green beans, ends trimmed, cut into 2-inch (5-cm) pieces
- 2 cups (290 g) fresh corn kernels, from 2 cobs (see tip on page 242)
- 3 tablespoons capers
- 2 tablespoons olive oil

  Kosher salt and freshly ground black pepper
- 2 medium 1-inch-thick (2.5-cm) swordfish steaks (1 lb/455 g)
- 1 teaspoon dried oregano
- 2 tablespoons chopped fresh flat-leaf parsley leaves

  Lemon wedges, for serving

HOW TO MAKE IT

Preheat your oven to 375°F (190°C), with a rack positioned in the center of the oven.

Combine the tomatoes, green beans, corn, capers, 1 tablespoon of the oil, 1½ teaspoons salt, and 1 teaspoon pepper in a 9 by 13-inch (20 by 30-cm) baking dish. Toss until evenly mixed.

Brush the fish with the remaining 1 tablespoon oil, and season on both sides with the oregano and 1 teaspoon each salt and pepper. Nestle the fish in the tomato-corn mixture. Cover with aluminum foil and bake until the swordfish is opaque throughout, 25 to 30 minutes.

Sprinkle the fish and vegetables with parsley. Serve hot with lemon wedges.

Coconut Curry Noodles with Shrimp and Napa Cabbage

MAKES DINNER FOR 4

I don't like doing any "work" while I eat dinner—for instance, sticking my hands in noodles to take off shrimp peels. So, I peel the shrimp tails off before cooking. Use your thumb to peel back one side of the tail, then pull gently on the end to unwrap the shell. Of course you can leave them on, that's up to you!

INGREDIENTS

- 2 tablespoons canola oil
- 1 bunch scallions, thinly sliced, some green parts reserved for serving
- ¼ cup (85 g) Thai red curry paste
- 1 tablespoon peeled and grated fresh ginger
- 2 cups (480 ml) chicken stock from Whole Poached Chicken (page 241), or Vegetable Stock (page 239)
- 2 (13.66-oz/403-ml) cans light coconut milk, shaken
- 2 tablespoons Asian fish sauce
- 1 small head napa cabbage (about 1 lb/455 g), finely shredded (about 6 cups)
- Kosher salt
- 8 ounces (225 g) rice noodles
- 1 pound (455 g) medium shrimp, peeled and deveined, tail-off
- 2 tablespoons fresh lime juice, plus wedges for serving
- Sliced fresh red chiles, for serving

HOW TO MAKE IT

Bring a large pot of water to a boil.

While the water comes to a boil, heat the oil in a separate large pot over medium heat. Add the scallions, curry paste, and ginger. Cook, stirring often, until the scallions are tender, 4 to 6 minutes.

Add the stock, coconut milk, and fish sauce and bring to a boil. Stir in the cabbage and return to a boil.

Salt the pot of boiling water and add the rice noodles. Cook according to package directions (it should take around 4 minutes) and drain.

Add the shrimp to the coconut-cabbage mixture, reduce to a simmer, and cook until the shrimp is opaque throughout, 1 to 2 minutes. Stir in the lime juice.

Drain and divide the noodles among four serving bowls and top with the stew. Serve with lime wedges, sliced red chiles, and the reserved scallion greens.

Seared Salmon with Sautéed Squash and Greens

MAKES DINNER FOR 4

It still amazes me how much flavor you can get out of a short list of ingredients. Plus, everything comes together quickly in one skillet, so you can sit down after only 20-ish minutes of cooking. Look for Bloomsdale spinach, which have larger leaves that come in a bunch (not in a clamshell). They have a deeper flavor than baby spinach, though that will work, too.

INGREDIENTS

- 3 tablespoons olive oil
- 4 (6-oz/170-g) pieces boneless, skinless salmon or Arctic char

  Kosher salt and freshly ground black pepper
- 3 medium yellow squash or zucchini (about 1 lb/455 g), cut into half-moons
- 3 garlic cloves, sliced
- 2 teaspoons fresh thyme leaves, plus more for serving
- 6 cups spinach leaves, stems trimmed, from a 12-oz/340-g bunch
- 1 tablespoon fresh lemon juice

HOW TO MAKE IT

Heat 2 tablespoons of the oil in a large nonstick skillet over medium-high heat. Season the fish on both sides with ½ teaspoon each salt and pepper. Cook the fish without turning, until the first side is golden brown and the edges are crispy, 4 to 6 minutes. Flip and cook until opaque throughout, 2 to 3 minutes more. Transfer the fish to a plate and keep covered while you cook the squash.

Wipe out the skillet with a paper towel. Heat the remaining 1 tablespoon oil in the skillet over medium heat. Add the squash, garlic, thyme, and ½ teaspoon each salt and pepper. Cook, tossing often, until the squash is just tender, 4 to 6 minutes. Stir in the spinach leaves in batches and cook until just wilted, about 1 minute more. Stir in the lemon juice.

Serve the fish on the squash, sprinkled with more thyme leaves, salt, and pepper, if you like.

Broiled Arctic Char with Marinated Cucumber and Radish Salad

MAKES DINNER FOR 4

Healthyish recipes are generally easy, pretty good for you, and quick. But as a rule, I stay away from making specific time promises because everyone moves at a different pace, and life gets in the way of a "20-minute recipe." But! I'm going to break my own rule and say that in 20 minutes or less you can have dinner on the table.

INGREDIENTS

1 English seedless cucumber (14 to 16 oz/400 to 455 g), very thinly sliced

8 radishes (about 8 oz/225 g), very thinly sliced

2 tablespoons olive oil

2 tablespoons fresh lemon juice

¼ cup chopped fresh dill, plus more for serving

2 tablespoons poppy seeds

Kosher salt and freshly ground black pepper

4 (6-oz/170-g) thin pieces skinless Arctic char

⅛ teaspoon cayenne pepper

HOW TO MAKE IT

In a medium bowl, combine the cucumber, radishes, oil, lemon juice, dill, poppy seeds, 1 teaspoon salt, and ½ teaspoon pepper. Let sit, tossing occasionally, until the cucumbers and radishes soften slightly, 10 to 15 minutes.

Meanwhile, cook the fish. Preheat your broiler to high. Line a baking sheet with aluminum foil and place the fish on top. Season with the cayenne pepper and 1 teaspoon each salt and black pepper. Broil until just barely opaque throughout, 3 to 5 minutes. Watch them like a hawk! They cook faster than you think and thin pieces cook super quickly.

Serve the fish with the cucumber-radish salad, sprinkled with dill, salt, and black pepper.

Modern Niçoise Salad for Two

MAKES DINNER FOR 2

This salad was inspired by a classic Niçoise. I love the combo of oily fish, salty olives, egg, and vegetables. But, I don't always have time to prepare vegetables for the traditional salad. Here, I answer the craving for those flavors with pantry and fridge staples. This recipe serves two because it's not suited to leftovers, but it'll double easily if you're serving four. If you're looking for a heartier salad, toss in some whole grains (page 236), thinly sliced raw green beans, or halved cherry tomatoes.

INGREDIENTS

- 4 large eggs
- 5 ounces (140 g) tender lettuce such as red leaf, Bibb, or Boston (about 6 cups)
- 1 (4.25-oz/124-g) tin oil-packed sardines
- ½ cup (85 g) chopped marinated artichokes
- ⅓ cup (50 g) Castelvetrano or Cerignola olives, pitted
- ¼ cup Cidery Dijon Vinaigrette (page 233)
- Flaky sea salt and freshly ground black pepper

HOW TO MAKE IT

Bring a small pot of water to a boil. Using a long-handled spoon, gently lower the eggs into the water. Roughly dropping it in can cause the shells to crack on the bottom of the pot.

Turn the heat down to a gentle simmer and set a timer for 7 minutes for soft boil, or 10 for hard boil. Carefully remove the cooked eggs and submerge in an ice bath or run under cold water until cool enough to handle. Tap the eggs gently on the counter and roll to crack the shells all over. Peel the shells off and cut each egg into quarters lengthwise.

Arrange the lettuce between two large shallow bowls. Divide the sardines, artichokes, olives, and quartered eggs between the two plates, then drizzle with the vinaigrette and season with ½ teaspoon flaky sea salt and a few grinds of pepper.

Fennel and Tomato-Poached Bass

MAKES DINNER FOR 4

Fennel is a polarizing ingredient—the anise undertone is a turnoff for many people. The key is to cook it well so that it turns sweet, not herbal. Add tender poached bass and a rich, tomatoey broth and you've got an elegant, simple stew that could convince the biggest fennel or fish hater. If you want to serve 6, add another 8 ounces (225 g) of bass. When you buy the fish, ask the fishmonger to remove any pin bones. (Those are the tiny bones that run through the center of the fish.) You can also thinly slice on either side of the spine to cut the bones out, or just pick them out as you eat.

INGREDIENTS

- 3 tablespoons olive oil
- 2 fennel bulbs (about 2 lbs/910 g), quartered and very thinly sliced
- 1 small onion, thinly sliced
- 4 garlic cloves, sliced
- 1 teaspoon dried oregano

    Kosher salt and freshly ground black pepper
- 4 cups (960 ml) chicken stock from Whole Poached Chicken (page 241), or Vegetable Stock (page 239)
- 1 (28-oz/794-g) can whole peeled tomatoes
- ¼ cup (40 g) pitted Kalamata olives, halved
- 1 bay leaf (optional)
- 1¼ pounds (570 g) skinless sea bass
- 2 tablespoons chopped fresh flat-leaf parsley leaves, plus more for serving
- 4 slices toasted whole-wheat country bread

    Shaved Parmesan cheese and lemon wedges, for serving

HOW TO MAKE IT

Heat 2 tablespoons of the oil in a large pot over medium-high heat. Add the fennel, onion, garlic, oregano, 1 teaspoon salt, and ½ teaspoon pepper. Cook, stirring often, until the fennel is soft, 10 to 12 minutes.

Add the stock, tomatoes, olives, bay leaf, and 1 teaspoon salt. Cover and bring to a boil over high heat. Add the fish and reduce the heat until the sauce is gently bubbling. Re-cover the pot and cook until the fish is opaque throughout, 3 to 5 minutes. Take the pot off the heat, remove and discard the bay leaf, and stir in the parsley.

Drizzle the bread with the remaining 1 tablespoon olive oil. Divide the fish and broth among four serving bowls. Sprinkle with generous slivers of Parmesan, extra parsley leaves, salt, and a few grinds of pepper. Serve with lemon wedges and the toasted bread alongside.

Balance is key. It's okay to dollop a spoonful of sour cream on your soup or add a few crumbles of bacon to your salad.

Winterfresh Tuna, Mushroom, and Shaved Fennel Salad

MAKES DINNER FOR 4

I call this salad winterfresh, because while it feels light and bright, the ingredients are actually all pantry staples or things you can get easily in the dark of winter. If you don't have time to make the marinated mushrooms, you can substitute store-bought ones, or add avocado or canned white beans instead. Use your mandoline (see tip on page 242) or the slicing disk on your food processor to cut the fennel into thin strips.

INGREDIENTS

- 1 large fennel bulb (12 to 14 oz/ 340 to 400 g), halved and sliced paper-thin (see tip on page 242)
- 3 tablespoons white wine vinegar
- 2 tablespoons olive oil

  Kosher salt and freshly ground black pepper
- 2 (6-oz/170-g) cans water-packed tuna, drained
- 1½ cups Marinated Mushrooms (page 222)
- 8 ounces fresh mozzarella, torn into bite-size pieces (about 2 cups/227 g)
- ½ cup (55 g) salted, roasted Marcona almonds, roughly chopped
- ⅓ cup Cidery Dijon Vinaigrette (page 233)

HOW TO MAKE IT

Toss the fennel with the vinegar, oil, ½ teaspoon salt, and ¼ teaspoon pepper in a large bowl. Use your hands to make sure it's well coated. Toss occasionally until the fennel is soft, 15 to 20 minutes.

Divide the fennel among four shallow serving bowls. Top with the tuna, mushrooms, mozzarella, and almonds, dividing them equally. Drizzle with the vinaigrette and sprinkle with the salt and a few grinds of pepper.

CHAPTER 9

Ah, dessert. My favorite chapter. When you've got an unabashed sweet tooth like I do, it's difficult not to end every meal with something sweet. Since balance is the key, I try to stick to one treat a day, max. And the recipes here vary from a glorified smoothie to decadent chocolate chip bars, so it's not *too* much sugar all the time.

This chapter is organized from quick one-off treats like Single-Serving Chocolate and Peanut Butter Cookie (page 200) to more involved desserts that serve a crowd like Triple Chocolate, Coconut, and Cashew Cookies (page 217).

What's essential is finding a rhythm that makes sense for you. Eating *Healthyish* allows for indulging occasionally—whether it's a treat for one, or a big batch of Ginger-Molasses Buckwheat Bars (page 214) to be shared with friends.

**Whole-Wheat Chocolate
Chip Cookie Bars**
PAGE 213

Banana-Date Shake

MAKES DESSERT FOR 2

This is the *Healthyish* version of a vanilla milkshake—swapping almond milk for whole cow's milk, and bananas for vanilla ice cream. It's lighter, sweeter, and less filling than a smoothie, but nobody's stopping you from calling it breakfast, if you like.

INGREDIENTS

2 frozen bananas

2 teaspoons date molasses, or 1 plump date, pitted (such as Medjool or Deglet Noor)

¼ teaspoon ground cinnamon

¼ teaspoon pure vanilla extract

1½ cups (360 ml) unsweetened almond milk

HOW TO MAKE IT

Combine all the ingredients in your blender, adding the almond milk last. Blend until smooth, and drink right away!

Chamomile Tea Affogato

MAKES DESSERT FOR 1

I'm a strict no-caffeine after 2 P.M. girl, so a classic affogato—espresso drizzled over a scoop of vanilla gelato—is out of the question after dinner. Instead, I go for a pour of flowery chamomile tea and a spoonful of tangy marmalade. Look for tea that doesn't have any natural flavors added.

INGREDIENTS

⅓ cup (75 ml) boiling water

1 chamomile tea bag

½ cup (100 g) vanilla frozen yogurt, ginger ice cream, or lemon sorbet

2 tablespoons orange marmalade

HOW TO MAKE IT

Pour the boiling water over the chamomile tea bag in a heatproof mug. Let steep 3 minutes, then remove the tea bag and squeeze it to get any tea out.

Place the frozen yogurt, ice cream, or sorbet in a small bowl or mug and then dollop with the marmalade. Pour the tea over the top and eat right away.

↖ **Chamomile Tea Affogato**

Single-Serving Chocolate and Peanut Butter Cookie

MAKES 1 COOKIE

Fair warning: Once you know how easy it is to make a single peanut butter and chocolate cookie, you might get in the habit of making one every single night. I originally developed this with almond butter, which tastes equally delicious but can be pricey. If you have a peanut allergy, any other nut butter swaps in perfectly well.

INGREDIENTS

- 2 tablespoons peanut butter, preferably natural
- 2 heaping tablespoons quick-cooking or instant oats
- 1 teaspoon confectioners' sugar
- ¼ teaspoon pure vanilla extract
- 1 tablespoon semisweet chocolate chips

  Flaky sea salt, for garnish (optional)

HOW TO MAKE IT

Stir the peanut butter, oats, sugar, and vanilla together in a small bowl until completely combined. Using your fingers, shape the mixture into a 2½-inch-wide (6-cm), ½-inch-thick (12-mm) disk. Press the tines of a fork into the top of the cookie. Chill on a parchment paper–lined plate in the freezer until firm, about 5 minutes.

Once the cookie is cold and hard, melt the chocolate in the microwave in 15-second bursts until stirrable. Spread half the chilled cookie with the chocolate, and sprinkle with a little flaky sea salt, if you like. The chocolate should set when it hits the cold cookie, but if it doesn't, you can return it to the freezer for a minute or two.

Raspberry and Shortbread Parfaits

MAKES DESSERT FOR 1 OR 2

This dessert is *Healthyish* eating at its core: Indulgence without going over the top. There's unsweetened whipped cream for richness, a tiny bit of sugar to sweeten crushed raspberries, and a crumbled cookie or two for crunch.

INGREDIENTS

- 1½ cups (6 oz/185 g) raspberries
- 1 teaspoon finely grated lemon zest
- ¼ teaspoon pure vanilla extract
- 1 teaspoon granulated sugar or pure maple syrup (optional)
- ¼ cup (60 ml) heavy cream, or ⅓ cup (75 ml) unsweetened whipped cream
- ¼ cup crushed cookies (shortbread or gingersnaps work well)

HOW TO MAKE IT

Mash the raspberries with the lemon zest and vanilla extract in a small bowl until they're saucy and mostly broken up. If the raspberries are very tart and you want the dessert to be sweeter, stir in a teaspoon of granulated sugar or maple syrup.

If you're whipping the cream yourself, use a balloon whisk to whip the cream in a medium bowl until you get soft peaks. It should take about 2 minutes. (A good pre-dessert workout!)

Layer half of the berries in a tall glass or bowl, followed by half of the whipped cream and crushed cookies, and then repeat with the remaining berries, whipped cream, and cookies.

Lemon Meringue "Pie" Sundaes

MAKES DESSERT FOR 2

My dad loves lemon meringue pie and I love to make it for him. But, I usually wait for a special occasion since it takes, oh, 6 hours start to finish. This easy dessert hits the same flavors but in a much quicker package. When fresh raspberries or blueberries are in season, they take this to a whole new level.

INGREDIENTS

2 tablespoons lemon curd

1 cup (200 g) vanilla frozen yogurt

2 hard meringue cookies

HOW TO MAKE IT

Microwave the lemon curd for 10 seconds, or until you can pour it easily.

Divide the frozen yogurt between two bowls. Crush one meringue over each bowl and then drizzle with the lemon curd. Eat immediately.

Fresh Fruit with Sour Cream Dipping Sauce and Pistachios

MAKES DESSERT FOR 2 TO 4

I love date molasses for its mellow sweetness. Look for it near the maple syrup at your grocery store or natural food market.

INGREDIENTS

- ½ cup (120 ml) sour cream
- 1 tablespoon date molasses or pure maple syrup
- ¼ teaspoon pure vanilla extract
- ⅓ cup (45 g) chopped roasted pistachios
- 3 tablespoons shredded sweetened coconut
- 1 pound (455 g) ripe fruit, such as strawberries, pears, bananas, mangoes, or peaches

HOW TO MAKE IT

Whisk together the sour cream, date molasses, and vanilla in a small bowl. In a separate bowl, mix together the pistachios and coconut.

Arrange the fruit on a serving plate with the sauce and pistachio-coconut mixture alongside. To eat, dip the fruit halfway in the sour cream, then roll in the pistachios and coconut. Use a fork or a skewer to dip hard-to-hold fruit such as bananas, mangoes, or peaches.

Easy Chocolate Buttons with Nuts and Dried Fruit

MAKES 16 BUTTONS

These are easy, elegant, and just decadent enough.

INGREDIENTS

- 9 ounces (255 g) chopped bittersweet chocolate
- ¼ packed cup (35 g) dried cherries
- ¼ packed cup (35 g) golden raisins
- ¼ cup (30 g) chopped roasted pistachios
- ¼ cup (40 g) sesame seeds

HOW TO MAKE IT

In a microwave-safe bowl, microwave the chocolate in 15-second bursts, stirring in between, until melted. Line a baking sheet with waxed or parchment paper and dab a tiny bit of chocolate underneath each corner of the paper to anchor it to the baking sheet.

Pour 16 scant tablespoon dollops onto the waxed paper. Use the bottom of a spoon or an offset spatula to gently spread the chocolate into 2½-inch (6-cm) rounds.

Mix the cherries, raisins, and pistachios in a small bowl and then sprinkle evenly over the chocolate. Follow with the sesame seeds, pouring evenly over each circle and covering any visible chocolate spots. Chill in the freezer 10 minutes before eating.

Store any extra buttons in an airtight container in the refrigerator for up to 1 week. Place in a single layer with parchment paper in between.

Stovetop Strawberry–Oat Crumble

MAKES DESSERT FOR 4

This summery dessert hits all the classic crumble flavors, but it comes together quickly on your stovetop so you don't have to turn on the oven. Oh, and don't skip the cornstarch—it's what helps the fruit juices thicken.

INGREDIENTS

- ½ packed cup (45 g) quick-cooking oats
- ¼ packed cup rolled oats, toasted
- 3 tablespoons light brown sugar
- 2 tablespoons all-purpose flour
  Kosher salt
- 6 tablespoons unsalted butter
- 1 tablespoon granulated sugar
- 1 pound (455 g) strawberries, quartered
- 8 ounces (225 g) raspberries
- 1 tablespoon cornstarch
- ½ cup (120 ml) Greek yogurt
- ½ teaspoon pure vanilla extract

HOW TO MAKE IT

To make the crumble topping, combine the oats, brown sugar, flour, and ⅛ teaspoon salt in a medium bowl. Melt 5 tablespoons of the butter and pour over the oat-sugar mixture. Stir until well combined. Cover and chill the crumble until solid, at least 30 minutes, or up to overnight.

Ten minutes before serving, combine the remaining 1 tablespoon butter and 2 teaspoons of the granulated sugar in a large nonstick pan over medium heat. Add the fruit and cook, stirring often, until the fruit has softened and released juices, 2 to 4 minutes.

Whisk the cornstarch with 1 tablespoon water and then scrape into the pan with the fruit. Cook, stirring constantly, until the fruit is very tender and the juices are bubbling and thick, 3 to 4 minutes more. Remove from the heat and cool slightly.

While the fruit cools, combine the yogurt, vanilla, the remaining 1 teaspoon granulated sugar, and ⅛ teaspoon salt.

Break the chilled crumble into small pieces with a spoon. Serve the fruit topped with the crumble and dolloped with the yogurt.

Whole-Wheat Chocolate Chip Cookie Bars

MAKES 24 BARS

These bars have a classic chocolate chip cookie flavor, but made *Healthyish* with whole-wheat flour. Instead of scooping individual cookies, you'll save time by scraping all the dough into a pan and cutting after baking.

INGREDIENTS

- 2¼ cups (9 oz/270 g) whole-wheat flour, spooned and leveled
- 1 tablespoon instant espresso powder
- 1½ teaspoons kosher salt, or ¾ teaspoon fine sea salt
- 1 teaspoon baking soda
- 1¼ cups (9 oz/250 g) packed light brown sugar
- ½ cup (3½ oz/100 g) granulated sugar
- 1 cup (2 sticks) unsalted butter, melted and cooled to room temperature
- 2 large eggs
- 2 teaspoons pure vanilla extract
- 12 ounces (340 g) chopped bittersweet chocolate, or 2 cups (345 g) bittersweet chocolate chips

HOW TO MAKE IT

Preheat your oven to 350°F (175°C), with a rack set in the center. Butter a 9 by 13-inch (20 by 30-cm) baking dish and line with parchment; leave a 2-inch (5-cm) flap overhanging on two sides. Set aside.

Whisk the flour, espresso powder, salt, and baking soda in a medium bowl. Set aside.

Whisk both sugars in a large bowl, making sure to break up any lumps. Add the melted butter and whisk vigorously for about 1 minute, until the mixture forms one mass. Scrape the sides of the bowl with a flexible spatula.

Whisk 1 egg into the sugar-butter mixture, stirring until it's fully mixed in. Whisk in the second egg and the vanilla and scrape the sides of bowl again.

Add the dry ingredients to the wet and stir with the spatula to fully combine until there are no streaks of dry ingredients left. Stir in the chopped chocolate or chocolate chips. Scrape the dough into the prepared pan and smooth into an even layer.

Refrigerate the dough for at least 10 minutes while the oven preheats. Bake, rotating halfway through, for 25 to 30 minutes, until the bars are golden brown and the crust is matte (not wet or glossy looking). Cool completely before cutting into 24 bars.

You can make and refrigerate the dough up to 2 days in advance, or freeze the unbaked bars for up to 3 months. They'll take longer to bake, 30 to 35 minutes.

Ginger-Molasses Buckwheat Bars

MAKES 12 BARS

Buckwheat bars may sound totally hippy-dippy, but these are the sleeper hit of this book. Trust me, you'll love them. Don't skimp on toasting the pecans— that nutty aroma balances out the sweet dough.

INGREDIENTS

- ¾ cup plus 2 tablespoons (1¾ sticks) unsalted butter, melted and cooled slightly, plus more for the pan
- ¾ cup (150 g) plus 1 tablespoon granulated sugar
- ¾ cup (95 g) whole-wheat flour
- ⅓ cup (40 g) buckwheat flour
- 2 teaspoons ground ginger
- 1 teaspoon kosher salt
- 3 large egg yolks
- ¼ cup (60 ml) unsulfured molasses
- 1 tablespoon finely grated orange zest
- 1 teaspoon pure vanilla extract
- 1 cup (4 oz/115 g) toasted pecans, finely chopped (see tip on page 242)
- ½ cup (70 g) dried cranberries, chopped
- ¼ teaspoon flaky sea salt

HOW TO MAKE IT

Preheat your oven to 375°F (190°C) with a rack set in the center.

In a large bowl, whisk the butter and ¾ cup (150 g) of the sugar until well mixed. Set aside while you measure the remaining ingredients.

In a medium bowl, whisk the whole-wheat flour, buckwheat flour, ginger, and kosher salt. Set aside.

Add the egg yolks, molasses, orange zest, and vanilla to the butter-sugar mixture and whisk until completely combined. Scrape the sides of the bowl and then whisk in the flour mixture. Scrape the bowl again and fold in the pecans and cranberries.

Scrape the dough into a nonstick 9-inch (23-cm) fluted tart pan or a 9-inch (23-cm) round springform pan and smooth into an even layer. (If you don't have a nonstick pan, butter and line the pan with parchment paper, then butter again.) Chill for at least 10 minutes, or up to overnight.

Sprinkle the remaining 1 tablespoon sugar evenly over the dough and tilt the pan to get an even coating. Sprinkle with the flaky sea salt. Place the pan on a baking sheet and bake, rotating front to back once, 24 to 28 minutes, until evenly golden brown with darker edges and starting to pull away from the sides of the pan. Cool on a wire rack for 30 minutes, then carefully remove from the sides of the pan. Cool completely, then cut into 12 wedges and serve.

Triple Chocolate, Coconut, and Cashew Cookies

MAKES 36 COOKIES

Here's my tip for being a better baker: Give everything a place. Use a spoon rest or the glass measuring cup that you melted the butter in to hold your spatula, and use a cutting board that's big enough to chop the cashews.

INGREDIENTS

- 1 cup (7½ oz/200 g) packed light brown sugar
- ¾ cup (6 oz/170 g) granulated sugar
- 1 cup (2 sticks) unsalted butter, melted and cooled to room temperature
- 2 cups (8½ oz/240 g) whole-wheat flour, spooned and leveled
- ¼ cup unsweetened natural cocoa powder (not Dutch process)
- 1 tablespoon instant espresso
- 1½ teaspoons kosher salt, or ¾ teaspoon fine sea salt
- 1 teaspoon baking soda
- 2 large eggs
- 2 teaspoons vanilla extract
- 1 cup (6 oz/170 g) semisweet or bittersweet chocolate chips
- 1 cup (6 oz/170 g) white chocolate chips
- 1 cup (5½ oz/155 g) roasted, unsalted cashews, chopped
- 1 cup (3 oz/85 g) unsweetened shredded coconut (toasted, optional; see tip on page 242)
- 1 teaspoon flaky sea salt, for sprinkling

HOW TO MAKE IT

If you're planning to bake the cookies right away, preheat your oven to 375°F (190°C) with a rack set in the center.

Whisk both sugars in a large bowl, breaking up any lumps. Add the melted butter and whisk vigorously for about 1 minute to dissolve the sugar in the butter. Scrape the sides of the bowl with a flexible spatula. Let sit at least 10 minutes while you measure out the rest of the ingredients.

Whisk the flour, cocoa, espresso powder, salt, and baking soda in a medium bowl. Set aside.

Whisk 1 egg into the sugar-butter mixture, stirring until it's fully mixed in. Whisk in the second egg and the vanilla and scrape the sides of the bowl again. Add the dry ingredients to the wet and stir with the spatula until there are no streaks of dry ingredients left. Stir in the chocolate chips and the cooled toasted cashews and coconut.

Refrigerate the dough for at least 10 minutes. Scoop the dough in 1½-ounce (43-g) portions with a spring-loaded scoop (or you can measure out generous 1 tablespoon scoops) onto parchment-lined baking sheets.

To bake right away: Space the dough balls 3 inches (7.5 cm) apart and sprinkle with the flaky sea salt. Bake the cookies for 8 to 11 minutes, until the edges are set and the cookies are matte (not wet or glossy looking). Remove from the oven and let cool on the baking sheets for 5 minutes, then transfer to a wire rack to cool completely.

To bake after the dough chills for 4 hours or longer (recommended): Place the scooped dough balls on a single baking sheet and wrap tightly with plastic wrap. Refrigerate for at least 4 hours and up to 3 days. You can also freeze the chilled balls of dough in an airtight zip-top bag for up to 1 month.

Thirty minutes before baking, preheat your oven to 375°F (190°C).

Space the dough balls 3 inches (7.5 cm) apart and sprinkle with the flaky sea salt. Bake the cookies for 14 to 18 minutes, until the edges are set and the cookies are beginning to turn golden brown throughout. Remove from the oven and let cool on the sheets for 5 minutes, then transfer to a wire rack to cool completely.

CHAPTER 10

Go-to Components

When coming up with a list of recipes for *Healthyish*, I was wary of making one of those books where you have to flip all over the place to create just one meal. Not to mention, there's a DIY mania for making things that frankly, I'd rather just buy. (I will never make my own kombucha, sorry!)

What makes something a "Go-to Component" as opposed to part of a recipe like sriracha mayo (page 170) is that it's versatile in pairing, or can be the base of a number of meals. A jar of pickles can be a mid-afternoon snack, dished up for a casual hors d'oeuvre, or chopped and tossed into a grain bowl. Similarly, a jar of Miso Butter (page 227) in your fridge is great on toast with an egg (page 36), but stir it into a bowl of whole-wheat pasta or layer it into a sandwich and you've got something entirely different.

These eighteen recipes are used frequently through-out the book. They're building blocks of my kitchen and I'm excited for them to be part of yours, too.

←
Marinated Mushrooms
PAGE 222

Pickles

I'm going to be real with you—I was always super intimidated by pickling. Boiling jars and needing to "sterilize" things? No, thank you. That's where quick pickling comes in. The shelf life isn't as long as traditional canning, but it's rare that any of these three recipes lasts longer than a week in my fridge, anyway.

Something tart and vinegary like a pickle is a great way to add a boost of acid to any salad, grain bowl, or toast. Play around by adding onions to your breakfast tacos, or marinated mushrooms on a breakfast bowl.

Lightly Pickled
Cucumbers
PAGE 224

Marinated
Mushrooms
PAGE 222

Quick-Pickled
Red Onions
PAGE 222

Quick-Pickled Red Onions

MAKES 2 CUPS

There are a lot of quick-pickled onion recipes out there that call for making brine and a lot of spices. I'm sure those taste wonderful, but when I'm talking quick, I'm talking 15 minutes. Of course these pickles do better the longer they sit, but the salt and vinegar works wonders in just 15 minutes of marinating.

INGREDIENTS

1 large red onion (12 to 14 oz/340 to 400 g), halved and thinly sliced or finely chopped (about 2 cups)

¼ cup (60 ml) red wine vinegar

2 teaspoons kosher salt

HOW TO MAKE IT

Put the onion in a resealable jar and then pour the vinegar and salt over the top. Seal the jar and shake vigorously to coat the onion with the salt and vinegar.

Continue to shake occasionally, until the onions are soft, at least 15 minutes. (You can do this in a bowl; stir frequently.) If you're planning to use the onions right away, you can use them now, but I like to let them sit at least an hour.

The pickles will keep refrigerated for up to 2 weeks.

Marinated Mushrooms

MAKES 3 CUPS

These live somewhere between a sautéed mushroom and a pickle. And, trust me, that's the best place to be. Use a damp paper towel to rub any dirt off the mushroom caps.

INGREDIENTS

¼ cup (60 ml) olive oil

3 garlic cloves, halved lengthwise

1 pound (455 g) button mushrooms, halved, or quartered if large

Kosher salt and freshly ground black pepper

¼ cup (60 ml) white wine vinegar

¼ small red onion, very thinly sliced

5 to 7 fresh thyme sprigs

1 teaspoon granulated sugar

HOW TO MAKE IT

Heat the oil in a large skillet over medium heat. Add the garlic and cook until golden brown and fragrant, 1 to 2 minutes. Use a slotted spoon to pull the garlic out and then add the mushrooms, 2 teaspoons salt, and ½ teaspoon pepper.

Cook, stirring once or twice, until golden brown and just barely tender, 3 to 5 minutes. There will be liquid left in the pan—this is okay! Remove the pan from the heat and stir in the vinegar, onion, thyme, and sugar.

Add garlic back to the mushrooms and cool completely. Transfer to an airtight container. The mushrooms will keep refrigerated for up to 1 week.

→ Marinated
  Mushrooms

Lightly Pickled Cucumbers

MAKES 48 PICKLES

If you're squeamish about the traditional boiling and sterilizing process, then this is the pickle recipe for you. You have to eat them more quickly than store-bought pickles, but that won't be hard. Plus, homemade pickles don't have food coloring like store-bought ones do. Use them in these recipes: Cucumber-Dill Tzatziki (page 234), My California BB Bowl (page 55), or Tangy Chicken Salad Tartine (page 87); but I promise you, they'll go fast as snacks.

INGREDIENTS

1   quart (960 ml) water

2   cups (480 ml) distilled white vinegar

¼   cup (35 g) kosher salt

1   tablespoon sugar

1   tablespoon black peppercorns

1   tablespoon mustard seeds

1   tablespoon coriander seeds

3   to 5 bay leaves

16 (4 lbs/1.8 kg) Kirby cucumbers, ends trimmed, cut into quarters lengthwise (or cut into 8 wedges if large)

¼   cup coarsely chopped fresh dill

HOW TO MAKE IT

Bring the water, vinegar, and salt to a boil in a large pot, stirring until the salt dissolves. Cool completely while you prep the remaining ingredients.

To mix the pickling spice, combine the sugar, peppercorns, mustard seeds, coriander seeds, and bay leaves in a small bowl.

Pack the cucumbers, dill, and pickling spice in heatproof jars, dividing them equally. Pour in the brine. Do your best to get as many cucumbers as possible in the jars so that the liquid comes up to the top. If it doesn't, top them off with water.

Cool completely, then seal well and refrigerate. They'll be ready to eat after 1 hour. The pickles will keep refrigerated for up to 1 month.

Compound Butters

A compound butter is as simple as stirring a few ingredients into butter. What's great is that it has the same long-lasting shelf life as a plain stick, but it adds so much more flavor to everything it touches.

← Lemony Parsley
Butter

↑ Miso Butter

Miso Butter

MAKES ¾ CUP BUTTER

As if butter weren't tasty enough, miso takes this to the next level. Use it on Miso-Butter Toast with a Nine-Minute Egg (page 36), stir it into pasta, or add a pat to hot soup.

INGREDIENTS

½ cup (1 stick) unsalted butter, at room temperature

¼ cup (70 g) white miso paste

HOW TO MAKE IT

Using a spatula, mix the butter and miso in a small bowl until thoroughly combined. Transfer to an airtight container and refrigerate for up to 1 month.

Lemony Parsley Butter

MAKES ½ CUP BUTTER

This is a great use for any unused herbs wilting in your crisper drawer. I like a straight-up parsley vibe, but any mix of soft herbs you have on hand—fresh tarragon, oregano, basil, or thyme—will do well.

I love stirring some into my scrambled eggs or melting a spoonful over a bowl of warm whole grains. You'll also need this to make Prosciutto and Cucumber Tartine (page 88).

INGREDIENTS

½ cup (1 stick) unsalted butter, at room temperature

½ cup (30 g) chopped fresh flat-leaf parsley

2 teaspoons finely grated lemon zest

1 teaspoon kosher salt

1 teaspoon freshly ground black pepper

HOW TO MAKE IT

Mix together the butter, parsley, lemon zest, salt, and pepper in a small bowl. Use it right away or store it in a jar in the fridge for up to 2 weeks.

Salad Dressings and Sauces

Homemade salad dressings are not only cheaper than store-bought, they're free of any extra chemicals or stabilizers. And, as with all processed foods, your own version will be lower in salt. My salad dressing recipes are what my friends most often ask for. Now they can be your secret weapon, too.

Dried Oregano Italian Vinaigrette

MAKES 2 CUPS VINAIGRETTE

I made this vinaigrette to go with my Old-School Pizzeria Salad (page 92) but discovered it adds a welcome brightness to any simple salad.

INGREDIENTS

1⅓ cups (315 ml) olive oil

1 cup (240 ml) red wine vinegar

2 teaspoons dried oregano

1 tablespoon kosher salt

1 tablespoon freshly ground black pepper

HOW TO MAKE IT

Whisk the oil, vinegar, oregano, salt, and pepper in a medium bowl until completely smooth and combined. Refrigerate the dressing in an airtight container for up to 1 month.

Shake it! You can also shake this dressing in the storage jar. Use an almost empty mustard jar or any clean one you've got.

Toasted Sesame and Miso Dressing

MAKES 1 CUP DRESSING

This dressing requires buying some special ingredients—but my guess is you'll be so addicted to this salty-sour umami bomb it'll become a house favorite. Use it in Brown Rice and Adzuki Bean Bowls (page 141) and, honestly, basically any salad you like.

INGREDIENTS

¼ cup (70 g) white miso

⅓ cup (75 ml) rice vinegar

¼ cup (60 ml) canola oil

¼ cup (60 ml) low-sodium soy sauce

1 tablespoon toasted sesame oil

HOW TO MAKE IT

Put the miso in a small bowl, then slowly whisk in the vinegar until you get a loose paste. Whisk in the canola oil, soy sauce, and sesame oil. Refrigerate the dressing in an airtight container for up to 1 month.

**Eggless Caesar
Dressing**
PAGE 232

**Dried Oregano
Italian Vinaigrette**
PAGE 229

Cidery Dijon Vinaigrette
PAGE 233

Creamy Tahini Dressing
PAGE 232

Toasted Sesame and Miso Dressing
PAGE 229

↑ **Sweet-Hot Peanut Sauce**
PAGE 233

Eggless Caesar Dressing

MAKES 2¼ CUPS DRESSING

My biggest complaint about Caesar dressing is figuring out how to spell Caesar. OK, maybe not. Truthfully, it's the garlic breath, the funky anchovies, and including a raw egg yolk.

This version goes lighter on garlic, keeps just enough anchovy to get that salty-savory balance, and skips the egg yolk altogether for a longer-lasting dressing.

INGREDIENTS

- 1 cup (4 oz/115 g) finely grated Parmesan cheese
- ¾ cup (180 ml) fresh lemon juice
- ½ cup (120 ml) olive oil
- 1 small head garlic (7 or 8 cloves), peeled
- ¼ cup (60 ml) Worcestershire sauce
- 3 tablespoons anchovy paste
- 1 teaspoon kosher salt
- 1 teaspoon freshly ground black pepper

HOW TO MAKE IT

Put all the ingredients in the bowl of your food processor or blender and process until completely smooth. Refrigerate the dressing in an airtight container for up to 1 week.

Creamy Tahini Dressing

MAKES 1¼ CUPS DRESSING

Don't worry about how tart this dressing is on its own. Tossed with greens or grains, the intensity mellows.

INGREDIENTS

- 6 tablespoons (90 ml) canola or vegetable oil
- ¼ cup (60 ml) tahini
- 2 tablespoons to ¼ cup (60 ml) water
- 1 teaspoon kosher salt
- ¼ teaspoon freshly ground black pepper
- ½ cup (120 ml) fresh lime juice
- 3 tablespoons mayonnaise

HOW TO MAKE IT

Whisk all the ingredients in a medium bowl until completely smooth and combined, starting with 2 tablespoons water and adding more to adjust consistency. Refrigerate the dressing in an airtight container for up to 1 month.

Sweet-Hot Peanut Sauce

MAKES 1¼ CUPS SAUCE

If you lived in the nineties, then you probably had at least one chicken skewer dipped in peanut sauce. Damn that was delicious. They were all the rage when I was growing up and then POOF—no more satay and sauce. I recreated a similar version here, and may I say, I think it's just as addictive.

Use this on Chicken and Greens Sauté with Peanut Sauce (page 151), but I'm pretty sure that almost any roasted veg would do well by it.

INGREDIENTS

½ cup (120 ml) smooth, natural peanut butter

½ cup (120 ml) water

3 tablespoons rice vinegar

1 tablespoon brown sugar

½ teaspoon kosher salt

½ teaspoon curry powder

½ teaspoon red pepper flakes

HOW TO MAKE IT

Put all the ingredients in the bowl of your food processor or blender. Process until completely smooth, scraping down the sides as necessary. Refrigerate the dressing in an airtight container for up to 1 week.

Cidery Dijon Vinaigrette

MAKES 1 CUP VINAIGRETTE

Every time I make a salad with this dressing, friends ask for the recipe.

INGREDIENTS

⅓ cup (75 ml) Dijon mustard

⅓ cup (75 ml) apple cider vinegar

1 teaspoon kosher salt

½ teaspoon freshly ground black pepper

½ cup (120 ml) olive oil

HOW TO MAKE IT

In a small bowl, whisk together the mustard, vinegar, salt, and pepper. Slowly drizzle in the oil, whisking constantly. Transfer to a jar or use immediately. Refrigerate the dressing in an airtight container for up to 1 month.

Shake it! You can also shake this dressing in the storage jar. Use an almost empty mustard jar or any clean one you've got.

Cucumber-Dill Tzatziki

MAKES 2 CUPS SAUCE

I can't get enough of this tangy sauce. If you make it for the Spiced Chicken and Chickpea Flatbreads with Cucumber-Dill Tzatziki (page 149) or Chips with Tzatziki and Tomatoes (page 74), save a little extra to add to savory morning grain bowls (pages 49–55) or a smoked salmon tartine (page 86). You can use regular cucumber, but I like the small Persian ones for a higher skin-to-flesh ratio.

INGREDIENTS

- 2 Persian cucumbers, cut into small dice (about 1¼ cups)
- 1 cup (240 ml) Greek yogurt
- ¼ cup (60 ml) fresh lemon juice
- ¼ cup chopped fresh dill, plus more for serving
- 1 teaspoon kosher salt
- 1 teaspoon freshly ground black pepper

HOW TO MAKE IT

Stir together all the ingredients in a small bowl. Use right away or transfer to an airtight container and refrigerate for up to 4 days. Just before serving, you might need to stir the tzatziki if the cucumber has exuded any water.

Boiled Whole Grains

Boiling grains (instead of using the absorption method) is a game-changing time-saver in kitchen. Not only do the grains cook in about half the time, but also you don't run the same risk of overcooking them to a sad mush.

A batch of whole grains in your fridge means you've got breakfast, lunch, and dinner ready for the week. Use them in a breakfast grain bowl (there are eight clever ideas starting on page 49), or top with an easy chicken and bok choy stir-fry (page 151).

What's great about these grains is that they are interchangeable. So if you've made a batch of barley, swap it in for the farro in Kimchi-Fried Farro (page 125). Same goes for the Summer Barley Bowl (page 96)—quinoa or brown rice would taste equally great.

Pearl Barley

MAKES 2¼ CUPS

INGREDIENTS

5   cups (1.2 L) water

1   cup (200 g) pearl barley, rinsed

1   teaspoon kosher salt

HOW TO MAKE IT

Bring the water to a boil in a large pot. Add the barley and salt and cover. As soon as the water returns to a boil, reduce to a strong simmer. Cook, covered, until the barley is tender, 20 to 25 minutes. (It's OK if the grains are still a bit chewy; you want them to stay this way!) Drain any extra liquid and cool to room temperature. Fluff with a fork and transfer to an airtight container. Refrigerate the barley for up to 5 days or freeze for up to 2 months.

Farro

MAKES 2¼ CUPS

INGREDIENTS

5   cups (1.2 L) water

1   cup (200 g) farro, rinsed

1   teaspoon kosher salt

HOW TO MAKE IT

Bring the water to a boil in a large pot. Add the farro and salt and cover. As soon as the water returns to a boil, reduce to a strong simmer, cover, and cook until the farro is tender, 14 to 18 minutes. (It's OK if the grains are still a bit chewy; you want them to stay this way!) Drain any extra liquid and cool to room temperature. Fluff with a fork and transfer to an airtight container. Refrigerate the farro for up to 5 days or freeze for up to 2 months.

Brown Rice

MAKES 2¼ CUPS

INGREDIENTS

5   cups (1.2 L) water

1   cup (190 g) short- or long-grain brown rice, rinsed

1   teaspoon kosher salt

HOW TO MAKE IT

Bring the water to a boil in a large pot. Add the rice and salt and cover. As soon as the water returns to a boil, reduce to a strong simmer. Cook, covered, until the rice is tender, 22 to 26 minutes. (It's OK if the grains are still a bit chewy; you want them to stay this way!) Drain any extra liquid and cool to room temperature. Fluff with a fork and transfer to an airtight container. Refrigerate the rice for up to 5 days or freeze for up to 2 months.

Quinoa

MAKES 2¼ CUPS

INGREDIENTS

5   cups (1.2 L) water

1   cup (170 g) quinoa, rinsed

1   teaspoon kosher salt

HOW TO MAKE IT

Bring the water to a boil in a large pot. Add the quinoa and salt and cover. As soon as the water returns to a boil, reduce to a strong simmer. Cook, covered, until the quinoa is tender, 10 to 14 minutes. (It's OK if the grains are still a bit chewy; you want them to stay this way!) Drain any extra liquid and cool to room temperature. Fluff with a fork and transfer to an airtight container. Refrigerate the quinoa for up to 5 days or freeze for up to 2 months.

Stocks

Take a stroll down the boxed stock aisle of your grocery store, and the ingredients in most will surprise you. Just one box can contain food coloring, way more sodium than I'm comfortable with, and "natural flavors," whatever that means. Making your own stock is work, yes, but the process is satisfying and you get something deeply flavorful, which can be the base of soups (pages 99–115), a saucy pasta (page 157), and more.

Vegetable Stock

MAKES 4 TO 5 QUARTS (DEPENDING ON THE SIZE OF YOUR POT)

A flavorful alternative to chicken stock for vegetarians.

INGREDIENTS

- 2 carrots, quartered
- 2 celery stalks, quartered
- 1 medium onion, peeled and quartered
- 1 head garlic, halved horizontally
- 10 fresh thyme sprigs
- 10 stems fresh parsley
- 10 to 15 black peppercorns
- 2 bay leaves
- 1 tablespoon kosher salt

HOW TO MAKE IT

Put all the ingredients in your biggest soup pot and fill the pot with water, making sure everything is covered and leaving 1 inch (2.5 cm) of room. Cover and bring to a boil over high heat. This will take around 30 minutes, but keep an eye on the pot.

When it's boiling, reduce the heat until the liquid is gently bubbling. Cook until the vegetables are completely soft, about 15 minutes more and up to 1 hour for a more flavorful stock. Set a fine-mesh strainer over a large bowl and carefully strain the stock into the bowl. Discard the solids.

Cool completely and refrigerate the stock in airtight containers for up to 1 week. You can also freeze the stock for up to 3 months.

Whole Poached Chicken with Bonus Stock

MAKES 6 CUPS COOKED CHICKEN MEAT; 4 QUARTS STOCK

No doubt, poaching a whole chicken and making stock is more work than buying it from the store. But, for the cost of the chicken alone, you get at least four quarts of stock for free. You can also make this with chicken bones. Cook for 1 hour, then strain.

INGREDIENTS

1   (4- to 5-lb/1.8- to 2.3-kg) chicken, patted dry and giblets removed

2   carrots, quartered (5 to 6 oz/ 140 to 170 g)

2   celery stalks, quartered

1   medium onion, peeled and quartered

1   head garlic, halved horizontally

10 fresh thyme sprigs

10 stems fresh parsley

15 black peppercorns

2   bay leaves

1   tablespoon kosher salt

HOW TO MAKE IT

First, poach the chicken. Put the chicken in a large soup pot. Top with the remaining ingredients and then fill the pot with water, making sure the chicken is covered and leaving just 1 inch (2.5 cm) of room between the top of the water and the lip of the pot. Cover and bring to a boil over high heat. This will take around 35 minutes, but keep an eye on the pot.

When it's boiling, reduce the heat until the liquid is gently bubbling. Cover and cook until the chicken is cooked through, 10 to 15 minutes more. Using tongs, transfer the chicken to a large bowl. Let the chicken cool until it's comfortable to handle. Pull the skin off and return it to the pot, then use your hands to pick the meat off the bones. Shred the meat into bite-size pieces. Set aside to cool, then refrigerate in an airtight container for up to 3 days.

To make the stock, return the bones and vegetables to the pot, then top the pot off with water (the level will have reduced once you've removed the chicken). Cook the stock for at least another 20 minutes and up to 2 hours for a more flavorful stock, then cool completely. Set a fine-mesh strainer over a large bowl and carefully strain the stock into the bowl. Discard the solids.

Refrigerate the stock in airtight containers for up to 1 week or freeze for up to 3 months.

Six Helpful Tips

TO CUT FRESH KERNELS OFF THE COB, stand a shucked cob on its tip in a large bowl. Use a serrated knife to cut in a sawing, downward motion as close to the cob as you can get. Run the blunt side of your knife along the cut cob to get any milky juices out, since these have intense corn flavor.

TO SLICE DELICATA SQUASH:
1. Slice ½ inch (12 mm) off the stem end (you do not have to peel the squash).
2. Halve the squash vertically.
3. Use a sharp-edged spoon or a melon baller to scoop the seeds out; discard.
4. Place the squash cut side down and slice it into ½-inch (12-mm) pieces.

TO TOAST NUTS:
Toast in a single layer at 375°F (190°C) for 7 to 10 minutes on a baking sheet. Cool completely before chopping.

TO PEEL GARLIC CLOVES QUICKLY, hit the garlic with the flat, wide side of your chef's knife. The skin should slip off easily.

TO SLICE FENNEL ON A MANDOLINE:
1. Slice the stem end off—about ¼ inch (6 mm) will do.
2. Make a handle: Cut off the long leafy fronds, but leave 2 inches (5 cm) of the darker green stems attached.
3. Halve the bulb from stem to tip of the fronds through the center of the bulb.
4. Slice the fennel on a mandoline, holding the "handle" to move the bulb up and down the blade.

TO TOAST COCONUT:
Spread it out over a baking sheet and toast for 1 to 2 minutes in a 350°F (175°C) oven or in your toaster oven. Watch carefully—it burns quickly!

Special Diets Index

special diets index

Gluten-Free, Dairy-Free, Egg-Free

Index

acknowledgments

This book wouldn't exist without the tireless effort, support, and guidance of Sarah Smith. You have been an incredible friend and partner in this journey, and I'm so excited to see where we go together. Thank you to Camaren Subhiyah for shaping my words and ideas into something better than I could have imagined. Deb Wood, you are a visionary. Thank you for translating my vision into a gorgeous reality. I am grateful to Abrams for giving me a home, and to the entire team for your collaboration and support.

Linda Pugliese, you are a badass photographer and I feel ridiculously lucky to have worked alongside you. What a joy to find a borderline telepathic collaborator on the shoot and for showcasing my food in the best light possible. Pearl Jones, you made every day on the shoot a delight and wo-manned the kitchen with grace, spunk, and verve. Alyssa Kondracki, your attitude is the tops—I think you ran to the store almost one hundred times and still kept a smile. June Xie, your testing skills and tireless work ethic were beyond. Thanks for all the factoids. Brittany Bennett, thank you for bringing energy and light to my kitchen and managing to simultaneously cook and chat alongside me any day we worked together. Thank you to Alex Brannian for helping source such beautiful props.

To all the cooks and editors I've worked alongside, thank you for supporting and inspiring me. Thank you to Sarah Copeland for giving me my first job as a recipe tester and intern, and for mentoring me these past eight years. Thank you to Lygeia Grace, Dawn Perry, and Charlyne Mattox. I can't imagine where I'd be without the three of you guiding and teaching me.

Blake MacKay, thank you for going above and beyond as a friend throughout this process and for helping shape *Healthyish* into what it could be. Annie Daly, the hippie to my new age witch, thank you for helping me find my voice and giving me guidance. Charlotte Hunt, to call you a sister isn't enough. Thank you for the love, and thank you for reminding me why I take on such crazy projects. Thank you to Danielle Vinocur for your support and care.

To the friends who've been there with me during this process and offered laughter, tears, and love: Vanessa Magro, Felicia Resor, Annie Boardman, Jess Thomas, Hanna McLaughlin, Cat Emil, Nora Gomperts, Alison Roman, Rebekah Peppler, Stephanie Sisco, Alexandra Repetto, Miles Kenyon, Jennica Johnstone, Arielle Schwartz, Matt Duckor, Steven Hopper, and Jennica Atkinson. I've leaned on each of you during this process (and missed a few social obligations . . .). For all this and more, thank you.

This book is dedicated to my parents, Maggie and Jim Hunt. Dad, you've inspired me to go for dreams I wouldn't have imagined I could have reached without your encouragement. Mom, you taught me how to cook, how to bake, and how to lean into my creativity. Thanks for your genes, thanks for the generosity, and thanks for the love. I am forever grateful.

about the author

Lindsay Maitland Hunt is a recipe developer and food writer living in Brooklyn, New York. A former editor at *Real Simple* and BuzzFeed Food, her clients have also included *Country Living*, Delish, Food Network, and *Food & Wine*. This is her first cookbook.

Editor: Camaren Subhiyah
Designer: Deb Wood
Production Manager: Alex Cameron

Library of Congress Control Number: 2016960984

ISBN: 978-1-4197-2656-9
eISBN: 978-1-68335-124-5

Printed and bound in the United States
10 9 8 7 6 5 4 3

Abrams books are available at special discounts when purchased
in quantity for premiums and promotions as well as fundraising
or educational use. Special editions can also be created to
specification. For details, contact specialsales@abramsbooks.com
or the address below.

ABRAMS The Art of Books
195 Broadway, New York, NY 10007
abramsbooks.com